The Internet
Research Guide

The Internet Research Guide

SECOND EDITION

Timothy K. Maloy

ALLWORTH PRESS
NEW YORK

04 03 02 01 00 99   5 4 3 2 1

Published by Allworth Press
An imprint of Allworth Communications
10 East 23rd Street, New York NY 10010

Cover design by Douglas Design Associates, New York, NY

Page composition/typography by Sharp Designs, Inc., Lansing, MI

ISBN: 1-58115-012-1

Library of Congress Catalog Card Number: 98-72763

Printed in Canada

Contents

III: Journalism Research

IV: Academic Research

V: Specialized Research

Appendixes

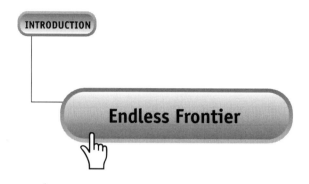

INTRODUCTION

Endless Frontier

In understanding the information resource that we call the Internet—particularly its World Wide Web section—it is helpful to look at a somewhat forgotten conceptual ancestor of the Net; the memex device.

In the mid-1940s, Vannevar Bush, a scientist, engineer, World War II military planner, government advisor, and visionary, conceptualized a futuristic information device—the memex—that he said would "give man access to . . . the inherited knowledge of the ages." Announced in an article entitled "As We May Think," published by *Atlantic Monthly,* the memex was concocted as a kind of desktop informational (i.e., microfiche) workstation with viewing screens, a keyboard, and various other machinery, such as levers, buttons, and switches.

Perhaps various parts of the memex sound familiar to you, the late twentieth-century reader. They should, not only for the use of keyboard and screen, but for what Bush said that this device would accomplish for the user.

Let us look a bit more at that.

This machine was to act as a private—albeit vast—library for its user. It would also act as a personalized device, such that when someone used the memex, it would form a set of "associative trails" for any particular research endeavor that would link various pieces of information.

These trails would be recorded so that future research into the same or a similar topic would be facilitated by having all these informational links on file.

Here is how Bush described his vision of what the memex would yield for humankind, in the "As We May Think" article:

Wholly new forms of encyclopedias will appear, ready-made with a mesh of associative trails running through them, ready to be dropped into the memex and there amplified. The lawyer has at his touch the associated opinions and decisions of his whole experience, and of the experience of friends and authorities. The patent attorney has on call the millions of issued patents, with familiar trails to every point of his client's interest. The physician, puzzled by a patient's reaction, strikes the trail established in studying earlier similar cases, and runs rapidly though analogous case histories . . . The chemist, struggling with the synthesis of an organic compound, has all the chemical literature before him in his laboratory . . .

The historian, with a vast chronological account of people, parallels it with a skip trail which stops only on the salient items, and can follow at anytime contemporary trails which lead him all over civilization at a particular epoch. There is a new profession of trailblazers, those who delight in the task of establishing useful trails through the common record.

According to Bush's biographer, G. Pascal Zachary, the *Atlantic* article sparked the imaginations of the time (mid-1940s) sufficiently that "As We May Think" was promptly excerpted by the Associated Press wire; written about and excerpted by *Time* magazine and the *New York Times;* and also reprinted in a condensed version by *Life* magazine, with drawings of this imagined device.

But though the memex has been a holy grail for informationalists since its conceptual inception—particularly for those in the library sciences—it has never actually been built. The idea, however, has remained and inspired many, including those in the computer sciences.

Now enter the Internet.

Similar in concept to the memex, the Net has begun implementing a framework enabling the Bush idea of technology that allows people the world over to store and consult "the records of the (human) race." The Internet, along with allied digital technologies such as desktop computers and the emerging breed of "information devices," is also much like the memex in that it has sparked imaginations in the current day, as the new millennium nears.

For any user of the Internet and its World Wide Web, the conceptualization of "associative trails" of information is closely comparable (with a few important differences) to the hyperlinking and bookmarking of documents and graphics that has become a reality for Netsurfers. The most striking similarity between the memex and the Net is their shared purpose—to help us find and access a world of information—which even at mid-century was a growing problem.

"Our libraries are filled to overflowing, and their growth is exponential, yet in this vast and ever-increasing store of knowledge, we still hunt for particular items with horse-and-buggy methods," Bush wrote, some years after his famous memex article. "As a result there is much duplication and repetition of research. We are being smothered in our own product." Bush goes on to lament that much information is "for all essential purposes, lost simply because we do not know how to find a pertinent item of information after it has become embedded in the mass."

So we have the conceptualization of the memex and the Net, both as instruments that can help us collect and collate information. But the amount of collective information available via the Internet and its various computer-server repositories around the world is vastly larger than perhaps even Bush or other thinkers might have ever imagined.

One estimate, as we approach the turn of the century, is that the amount of information on the Internet encompasses nearly 500 million pages. Additionally, the Net is an entirely new concept in that it allows for communication among users who can not only communicate via electronic mail, but also exchange large files of information.

Furthermore, there is the question of real-time information. A person can listen to radio stations the world over via the Net, download breaking news, and even watch many events live.

So we see that as the twentieth century turns towards the twenty-first, the long-considered dream of persons such as Bush and many others (to collect and make available a world of knowledge (is actually, and profoundly, coming at last to fruition.

About this Book

The idea of having an Aladdin's lamp that would give access to the information of the entire world has always stoked the fires of human imagination. Now, with the growing use of the Internet, we see the beginning of the implementation of this idea and how it is starting to enrich and help fuel the engines of the human mind.

This revised edition of *The Internet Research Guide* will help steer you in your search for information in the vast region of cyberspace and maybe even lead you to knowledge. Ultimately, the task is yours to undertake. In the pages that follow, you will find everything you need to know about how the Internet is being used for informational purposes. In addition to various chapters on search strategies and the various search engines and how to use them, this book also specifically looks at how three main categories of Netsurfers—business users, academics, and journalists—are making practical use of the Net. The main sections will be divided into these three categories and will explain how these professions (business, academia, and journalism) are using the Internet for research.

The fourth section of this guide tells you about some of the specialized items that you can look up on the Net, including e-mail addresses, phone numbers, maps, directions, and even where to find the perfect martini when traveling in the big city.

In the appendixes, *The Internet Research Guide* outlines for the new user how to connect with the Internet and navigate it successfully, and suggests where to visit for many types of information.

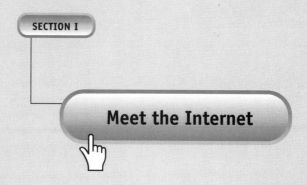

SECTION I

Meet the Internet

CHAPTER 1

Why You Should
Use the Internet

E VER ASK YOURSELF: *Why the Internet? Why should I use it? Why was it invented?*

The Internet—a global network of computers—has become today's hot topic. It has suddenly gone from a somewhat esoteric communication system used solely by scientists and academics to a household buzzword. Who hasn't been asked for their e-mail address? Who hasn't been told a lengthy URL (uniform resource locator) for finding something topical on the Internet? "Oh yeah, it's on the Web. Just look it up at *www.blah blah blahh . . .*" Who hasn't heard the joke: "On the Internet no one knows you're a dog." (Although, as we approach the year 2000, this mid-nineties *New Yorker* cartoon is already becoming dated.) Or who hasn't thrown up their hands at some point and said, What are these people talking about? What are FTP and HTTP protocols, newsgroups, domain names, listservs?

Well, no need to worry. These are all questions we'll be answering in full. When it comes to using and navigating the Internet we are all (as the title of a best-selling Internet book suggests) "big dummies"— in the beginning and even in the middle. It's hard to remember it all, and there are always new things to learn about and from the Internet.

But enough of that.

Why should you, as an individual (student, academic, writer, corporate researcher, or information specialist) be interested in spending long hours hunkered down in front of a computer screen, surfing through a global computer system? Or, to put it more succinctly:

Why should you use the Internet?

The answer is simple. Because the Internet is the "Mother of All Information Sources." You can quote me on that.

Forget (for now) trying to understand the technological workings of the Internet—transfer control protocols and packet switching networks and all that. What you really need to understand about the Internet isn't so much the technology behind it as what is accessible through the Net.

It is nothing short of the world's biggest library.

Through the Net, you can visit online the majority of the libraries at universities around the world, great and small, as well as many special libraries. Why, even the National Library of Medicine is on the Net. You can also access virtually every federal agency, all the state governments in the United States, and thousands of cities and towns.

You can read books courtesy of Project Gutenberg, and you can look at paintings in the Louvre or at the Los Angeles Art Museum, or the Warhol Museum in Pittsburgh, Pa., for that matter. There is, in short, information animal, vegetable, mineral, and medical on the Net.

But if the Internet and its World Wide Web is like a large (and I do mean large) library—and libraries have always been the collection point for information—what makes the Net different from a standard library? What makes the informational resources available through the Net so special compared with standard library resources?

Well, whereas traditional types of libraries have individual, separate books, papers, and documents, and so forth, the Internet is the equivalent of connecting all the books, papers, journals, and documents together. And besides having interconnections (hypertext links) between all the available resources, you also get color pictures, sound, and very soon, real-time digital movies that all accompany the text that you read in this new type of library we call "the Internet."

Though the Internet was once the domain of scientists and academics, it has changed dramatically during the 1990s to also become very much a place of business. Corporate researchers go online to keep track of what the competition is doing—by monitoring online news, company Web sites, online chats, and many other Net-based information resources.

These days, it is a matter of course for an average individual investor to go online and check his or her stock portfolio, financial news, and maybe even trade stock and bonds. You can shop for a mortgage or hunt for employment. All of which demonstrates that whether it's corporate research, individual investment, or other business usage, there is much that can be found on the Net.

The implication of all this online information is that you, as a researcher, can immediately access primary source material such as the full text of legislation, congressional debates, recent Supreme Court Decisions, or the U.S. Federal Code, almost anywhere, anytime. This also goes for a great deal of information from governments around the planet, as well as the United Nations.

In the case of Washington, D.C., the Internet alleviates in one stroke much of the need for a physical research presence. This means you don't have to maintain an expensive Washington news bureau or corporate office (unless you choose to for the prestige). And you don't have to completely rely on expensive research tools and databases such as Lexis/Nexis.

While this information is actually stored in computer servers at many different geographical locations, the Net allows you to reach out into the world and get this information—almost instantly. It is all interconnected. Internet philosopher John Perry Barrow has said of this network, "It is rather like the Buddhist notion of Indra's net—an infinite grid of pearls, each of which reflects perfectly the image of every other pearl in it."

All this decentralized communication bodes well for breaking up the office monotony a bit. In fact, with Internet-based research, you don't even need an office at all. You can use a computer and modem to carry on research from your home. For larger organizations that aren't about to close down their offices, this means that you don't always have to send people out into the field for research. Or, if you do have staff that is out-of-pocket, they can easily communicate with the office from far afield. And for the individual, the Net presents the possibility of communicating with your office or with the world-at-large from the comfort of home. While this phenomenon—known as telecommuting—is already well known, we are likely to see a lot more decentralized workforces in the coming years, courtesy of the Internet.

All this can sound like a lot of hype—"information superhighway" and all that. The Internet, and the information it makes accessible, isn't quite a superhighway, as it is often a little too disorganized. (This is also what makes the Net different from a standard library.) And for many types of connections, the Net is rather too slow (as of this writing) to be considered a superhighway. But, as you will see, the Internet will prove indispensable to your research, writing, communications, and even your marketing.

So forget all the hype and hackneyed clichés and just think of the Internet as the way to access your personal *Encyclopædia Britannica* magnified by a million. In fact, the *Encyclopædia Britannica* itself is on the Net (*www.eb.com*), along with a number of other famous reference books. Think of the Internet as a way to interview sources worldwide via e-mail; think of it as a way to connect your staff; think of it also as a way to repackage and deliver much of the print information you already publish. And, not least, think of the Internet as a way to increase your interaction with the world you live in.

Why Was the Internet Invented?

Now that you understand that the Internet is like a vast library, the next thing to understand is that the Internet doesn't really exist.

What?!

Well, yes, it exists, but it isn't a commercial entity like America Online or the Microsoft Network. There is no one to call and complain to.

No one owns the Internet!

There is no centralized profit motive.

There is no attempt at customer satisfaction.

What the Internet is, is a "network of networks." By common consensus, many organizations and persons have used the Internet to link their myriad computer networks, thus improving their mutual transfer of information. And in the same spirit that universities, libraries, museums, and corporations join the Internet network, they can also leave whenever they want. Right now is a golden period in Net history, because many different entities are rushing to join, and, therefore, there is more information available than ever before.

This is also a unique period because almost everything you access through the Net is free; that is what differentiates the Internet from commercial online services. Right now, one could say the slogan is "Be there or be square" for many organizations providing information through the Net. Later on, they may wonder if it is worth the cost of giving away information just to be a player. But then also, many information publishers of all kinds—including book publishers—will find eventually that they can make a lot of money disseminating information through the Internet. In part, this is dependent on working out a "microtransactions" scheme, whereby an information publisher gets paid every time someone browses their information. Even if a user only pays pennies at a time (which will probably be the going rate) there are so many people bound to be using the Net in the future, these pennies could rack up into millions of dollars.

One could, however, conjecture on potential Internet commercial opportunities forever. Some experts believe that the Internet will be the death of the online services. Others point to the fact that the "pie" just seems to keep growing in terms of persons getting online, and that there are more than enough customers to go around for both the online services and the Internet access providers.

Now for a bit more Internet history.

The Internet had its origins as a computer communications network set up by the Department of Defense (DoD). Defense researchers developed something called the ARPANet. It was designed as computer network that would maintain communications even if individual locations were destroyed by nuclear attack. This was done by using transfer control protocol/Internet protocols (TCP/IP) that led to the creation of a decentralized communication system that would "dynamically reroute" messages around destroyed or disabled sites. This is known as "packet switching."

NASA and the National Science Foundation (NSF) continued research on this same kind of "packet switching" network. The NSF fostered faster communications between its supercomputer centers so that scientists in the United States and abroad could make use of supercomputing resources without actually being at a supercomputer center. This research by DoD, NASA, and the NSF resulted in what has become known as that world-straddling, monolithic noun—*the Net.*

The growth has been startling. In 1981, there were only about 200 "host" computers on the Internet. By the beginning of the 1990s, there were 300,000, and in 1995, there was an estimated 3.2 million host computers on the Net.

Until several years ago the Internet had largely served as a communications medium for academics and scientists—in part, it was just a big inter-office mail system among colleges. Many of the customs of the Net come from this academic origin.

The Internet came to popular attention several years ago with the creation of the World Wide Web (WWW or "the Web") by European scientists at the European Particle Physics Laboratory (CERN), allowing physicists worldwide to more easily exchange and access information. The subsequent creation of graphical Web "browsers" such as Mosaic and Netscape made the WWW part of the Internet very easy to use and led to the explosion in Net usage and subsequent interest these last several years. These browsers enable those using the Internet to "read" documents that are on the World Wide Web section of the Net. The interface mostly involves "point-and-click" navigation that is a lot easier than the previous necessity of keyboarding in arcane UNIX commands.

CERN's statement of purpose for the World Wide Web (WWW) is as follows:

> To allow information sharing within internationally dispersed teams, and the dissemination of information by support groups. Originally aimed at the High Energy Physics community, it has spread to other areas and at-

tracted much interest in user support, resource discovery and collaborative work areas. It is currently the most advanced information system deployed on the Internet, and embraces within its data model most information in previous networked information systems.

What they don't mention is that the Web is "cool" looking, with multimedia documents that can carry text, graphics, and even sound.

And that is it, in a nutshell.

Now, everybody is jumping on the bandwagon, both in using and in providing information via the Internet. College students routinely access the Internet courtesy of their schools, and they often put up their own personal home pages. Companies are rushing to have home pages on the WWW to act as "electronic storefronts" and information resources. The U.S. government has been reinventing itself by providing comprehensive access to vast amounts of information. And even newlyweds are announcing their new status with Net pages.

A *USA Today* reporter, amazed at this new medium, said of the Internet's burgeoning growth: "Welcome to the Internet, an organism unlike any in history."

CHAPTER 2

The State of Research

In the summer of 1997, an unusual fact-finding contest took place that aptly demonstrated that the Internet had really come of age as a research tool.

The contest?

It required producing a white paper (a report) on Russian organized crime by using something known as Open Source Intelligence (OSINT), which in this case meant access to news and other types of public information that was easily available on the Internet. Classically, in the intelligence field, the use of OSINT involves anything from combing through newspapers worldwide to interviewing business travelers, tourists, refugees, and immigrants, and working with academics and scholars to study various hot and current topics.

The OSINT Internet contest was between British graduate students and veteran British intelligence analysts who have spent their career gleaning facts and creating a coherent picture out of many different sources of information. Sponsoring the contest was The International Centre for Security Analysis (ICSA), King's College, London.

A researcher at the ICSA, Lorenzo Valeri, wrote an article shortly after the contest for *Jane's Intelligence Review,* a well-regarded journal that noted how the Internet may soon make the use of Open Source Intelligence a common practice among intelligence analysts.

"The Internet is probably the epitome of the information revolution." wrote Valeri. "Only a few years ago it was unknown outside a limited circle of specialists, Today, Internet connectivity is growing exponentially."

He cautioned, however, that information overload is currently one of the defining features of the Net, and that "users complain of the difficulty of extracting useful signals from background noise." What is needed, before intelligence agencies start rushing to use the Internet, Valeri noted, "are well-formulated procedures and strategies that make best use of the Net and which incorporate it into existing intelligence processes."

Thus Kings College held this contest in order to see what kind of strategies are best for using the Net. The rub for this particular Internet information hunt—each side (divided into five teams of two persons each) was given only six hours to surf the Net and write a two-thousand word report. Valeri reported that the different research strategies adopted by each team provided "interesting perspectives on methods of approach for using the Internet."

> As the topic was handed out, each team spent some time designing a rough outline of the paper, . . . all immediately had ideas of where to start looking beyond [just] the main search engines.
>
> . . . each competitor knew where to start to look as they regularly used the Internet in their academic or professional occupations. Each member of the team, however, concentrated on a particular aspect of the topic such as Russian organized crime in general or Russian activities in the U.K.

Three of the teams spent almost half of the allotted time with each member surfing the Net in order to collect information. As the team members Netsurfed, each would bookmark relevant Web sites and take various text from these sites for insertion into word processor notepads. The various members of each team then began to fill out the research outlines they had initially prepared, with attention paid to avoiding inconsistencies and duplications. The other two teams split duties, with one member drafting the report while the other performed Internet research.

"As information was collected, it was immediately assessed and fed inside the rough outline," Valeri wrote. "Consequently a rough version of the final paper was written in quite a short amount of time. The rest of the time was devoted to finding more specific information about particular aspects."

Valeri reports that during this second phase, each team member of these two particular research teams went back on the Net to narrow down their information hunt. Also, though each team had different methods of researching and writing, there was a great similarity in the sources of information that they used from the Internet, i.e., all teams visited many of the same Web sites. In the end, each team was judged as having produced a white paper that was of above-average quality for what is considered the standard for this kind of report.

Valeri reported, however, something very interesting regarding which papers were judged as being superior to others in the contest. "It was striking that, in this competition, civilian graduate students managed to outperform intelligence professionals." Valeri wrote. "Although all competitors were familiar with the Internet and used to searching it, there were clear differences in research strategies which affected the quality of the product."

Valeri points out at the conclusion of his article "that the Internet, if properly used, can be a cost-effective tool to help analysts quickly prepare intelligence briefs on topics that suddenly become relevant."

CHAPTER 3

Research Methodology: Animal, Vegetable, Mineral

While the Internet is among the top methods for researching almost any subject, the Net should not serve as your exclusive method of research. Instead, the Net should serve as but one arrow (one of your most deft) in your entire quiver of research methods. Put simply, you can find an enormous amount of information on the Internet, but you should also consider supplementing that with a trip to a traditional library, depending on how thorough the scope of your research is.

Search Engines

"Search engines" are a fundamental tool for the Internet researcher. Essentially, these engines are large-scale indexed databases that have been compiled after "spider" programs have crawled through the vastness of the Internet and recorded the contents of each page visited.

All search engines work in basically the same way: you enter a word or phrase describing what you are hunting for, and the search engine goes hunting through its indexed database for word, phrase, or "concept" matches. Upon completion of its search, the software presents you with a list of what it has discovered, including the Internet addresses of the source materials. One clicks on an address and is taken to the source. Some of the top Internet search engines include AltaVista, HotBot, Lycos, Excite, and Yahoo.

Here are some thoughts about what the Internet is strong on:

- Access to government documents and publications that are either difficult to find or simply unavailable from one's local library.
- Special online versions of traditional print materials—EDGAR (Securities and Exchange Commission company information), *Encyclopædia Britannica*, THOMAS (Library of Congress), Congressional Record, and Electronic Newsstand which offers reprints of some (but not all) articles from major periodicals and newspapers.
- Unique materials available only on the World Wide Web—software and shareware, electronic journals and hypertext versions of periodicals that feature different content than their traditional-media counterparts.
- Press releases and media contacts—the Internet is a vast source of "unmediated" news.

Top Ten Tips for Internet Researching

Because one's expectation of "the information superhighway" can easily get overblown by hype and news media reports or by advertising that exaggerates the ease of Internet usage, one should keep a level head on their shoulders as they approach the Net. And as in any other research endeavor, adopting a formal strategy will maximize results. Here are some tips for starting your Internet research:

1. Ask yourself, Exactly what information is being looked for? Is it legal, scientific, literary, or artistic? Is the topic animal, vegetable, or mineral? What is the subject category? Who may be the author of what you are looking for? What is the date of publication? Is the material from a book, magazine, scientific paper, or abstract? Are you looking for an electronic publication or a paper publication that may also exist in digital form on the Net?

2. While finding particular information on the Internet is exactly what you are attempting, do you know that this information is actually on the Internet? Have you heard or read that it is on the Net? Did

your boss say it is on the Net? The more that you can find out about where it might reside on the Internet, the easier it is to find. Did you run across a certain resource during earlier Internet research that you are now trying to track again?

3. What may be the "keyword" or "keywords" of what you are looking for? This is necessary, if not crucial, when using Internet search engines.

4. As much as possible, familiarize yourself with what resources and organizations are on the Internet. There are a number of Internet-based and hard copy directories that cite specific resources. With regard to Internet-based directories, there are a number of top spots to begin your research. For instance, Yahoo is one of the premier Internet directory resources.

5. With regard to staying current in your subject area and familiarizing yourself with what's out there, one should join relevant subject-related Listservs (mailing lists) and Usenet newsgroups. There are thousands of them to pick from, and they cover every subject imaginable, from biology to body piercing. Also, there are a variety of electronic newsletters, such as Gleason Sackman's *Net Happenings Digest* (*http://scout.cs.wisc.edu/scout/net-hap/*), which publishes new sites categorized by topic on a continual basis, or the similar and equally good *Netsurfer Digest* (*www.netsurf.com/ nsd*), published by Netsurfer Communications.

6. As you familiarize yourself with the Net, start "bookmarking" your favorite and most helpful research home pages. The bookmark function is contained in all Web browsers and allows the Netsurfer to compile a list of Net addresses for easy return. For example, if you often use U.S. Government information in your research, then you would want to bookmark THOMAS, the Internet guide to the government hosted by the Library of Congress.

7. After you have familiarized yourself with the myriad of informational resources on the Internet and are quite knowledgeable about all the different Internet guides and search engines, you should maintain a high degree of discipline when researching. Remember to stick to the topic you are looking for. With an estimated 500

million pages on the World Wide Web portion of the Internet alone, it is easy to find yourself sidetracked as you are led down the garden path away from your original topic. The Internet is very Victorian in its eclecticism, and that is both its beauty and its danger. So stay focused and don't wander from Civil War history into the War of the Roses when you stumble into a university history department somewhere on the Internet.

8. Closely related to the need for discipline is the continual willingness to scrap your initial Internet research findings that aren't yielding good results and use different keywords or try other Web sites (and sometimes Gopher and FTP sites) than those you have been looking at. Let's say, for example, you are looking for cultural information on gay events, happenings, and writings. Do you use the word "gay" or "homosexual" as a keyword? If you use just the word "homosexual," you are likely to run across scientific information pertaining to human sexuality. If the initial information you are finding is irrelevant, then go back and start again. Also, if you have passed by a home page that now seems more relevant to your research, use the "back" arrow function on your Web browser to go back and look at that page again.

9. What happens when you can't find the answer to your question? Here are some suggestions: Look at your resources. Are they appropriate to your search needs? For example, are you trying to search for a piece of legislation the contains the word "communications?" If you use any of the larger search engines for this keyword, you will get thousands more "hits" than you want. Instead, go to a specific Internet resource related to the subject (i.e., legislation), such as THOMAS at the Library of Congress. In general, as you begin your research, try to find the particular resource related to your query. In a traditional library, you wouldn't use a periodical guide to look for books. Using the right resource holds true both on and off the Net.

10. How do you know when you have successfully concluded your research on the Internet? This can be problematic, in part because of the large scope of information regarding some topics on the

Internet. But often, you know that your search is over for the simple reason that you have answered the question that you first posed: What are the opening lines of the Gettysburg Address? What year did Columbus discover America? What did the Supreme Court decide regarding abortion in *Roe vs. Wade*? In Internet research, as in other mediums, the question of concluding your research is often inherent in the question you posed to begin with.

Information Hunting

Here is a quick Internet road map for company information, government data and legislative documents, news clippings, and public relations releases.

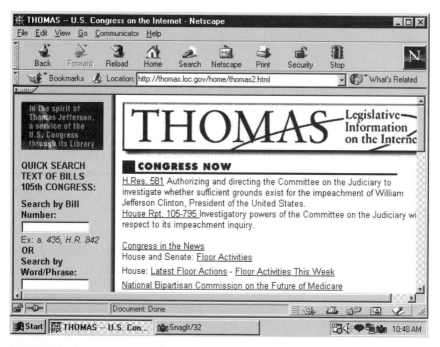

THOMAS is the gateway to information from the U.S. Congress.

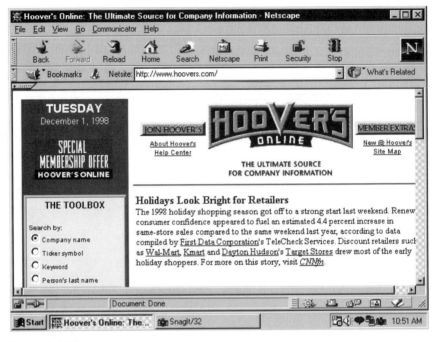

Hoover's Online

Business and Finance

For basic information about corporation finances "EDGAR" (electronic data gathering and retrieval) at the Securities and Exchange Commission can be accessed at *www.sec.gov/edgarhp.htm.* Hoovers Online (*www.hoovers.com*) is another site that provides data about businesses, and, while it does have a premium "members only" section, there is also a great deal of company information available in the "free" area.

The ups and downs of the stock market can also be tracked via the Web. The New York Stock Exchange is at *www.nyse.com,* the American Stock Exchange at *www.amex.com,* and NASDAQ at *www.nasdaq.com.* For demographics and marketing information, go to American Demographics Inc. *(www.marketingtools.com).*

Government Data and Legislative Info

For government data and legislative information, THOMAS (*http://thomas.loc.gov/*) is probably any researcher's single best starting point,

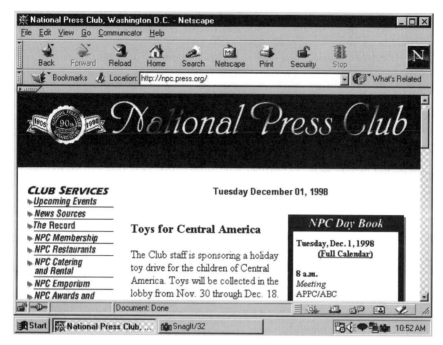

National Press Club

providing government documents with the primary information related to congressional affairs (legislation and official record). Another excellent starting point for all things governmental is the White House (*www.whitehouse.gov*), which is particularly good for press releases and policy pronouncements from the Chief Executive. Both the THOMAS and White House Web sites act as good gateways to the entire federal government, with the latter having a link to each agency at its site.

Fed Stats (*www.fedstats.gov*) contains a handy collection of URLs for all federal agencies that collect statistics. At the Department of Commerce site (*www.doc.gov*) one is provided with a vast array of statistical data and government reports on business (domestic and international), census, and even weather.

News Services, Papers, and Clippings

The National Press Club (NPC) homepage (*http://npc.press.org*) is one of the single best spots for embarking on Internet-based research of any kind, and includes news clippings and more. Also at this Web site is a daybook of events at the prestigious NPC. The famous Yahoo Internet directory has a free daily news feed that is mostly comprised of Reuters wire copy, but includes other sources as well. News can be accessed at *http://yahoo.com/headlines/*. Researchers should also visit Cable News Network Interactive (*www.cnn.com*), one of the superior online news Web sites.

For a gateway to international news sources, go to the home page of *Editor and Publisher* magazine (*www.mediainfo.com*), a top trade publication for the journalism profession. This Web site contains links to more than 2,000 online newspapers around the world and, for the United States, has links to television stations that have Web sites.

NewsPage (*www.newspage.com/*) promotes itself as the Web's leading source of daily business news, and it probably is, with thousands of stories from hundreds of different information sources. NewsPage has both a free and "members only" pay component (cost is relatively cheap). BusinessWire (*www.businesswire.com*) is another business news provider.

Press Releases can be found at PR Newswire (*www.prnewswire.com*). This is the online version of the well-regarded public relations wire that is used in thousands of news rooms and news bureaus. Company news releases can be found here quickly using keywords.

CHAPTER 4

The Top Search Engines

E ver ask yourself, How do those darn search engines work? Why are they so fast—or so slow—and how is it they sometimes come up with exactly what you are looking for, or sometimes come up with literally 90,000 (or more) hits for various Web sites almost totally unrelated to your search?

What one should understand foremost about search engines is that they are *dumb*, after a manner of speaking. They don't know what you are looking for as such; rather, they simply take a keyword or set of keywords and look for the occurrence of those words. And where do they look for those words? Well, not actually on the Net itself.

What? you ask, But Internet search engines are supposed to search the Net!

Well, here's what they actually do.

How Search Engines Work

Search engines essentially have three component parts to them. The first, and in many ways the most important part, is the spider program, which sends digital robots spidering through the Net. There, they methodically record and index Web pages, starting with the Uniform Resource Locator (URL), and then the page title, its first paragraph, and so on, eventually spidering each and every word on every Net page at a given Web site.

And a spider actually does each page very quickly. But given that there are hundreds of millions of Web site addresses (URLs) on the Net, it takes a spider a long time to cover the waterfront, as it were. Once a page is "spidered," that program saves the recorded index (rather than the actual page) to a database created by that search engine. So the second component of that engine is the database, and it is here that many engines lay claim to their prowess, saying "I have the biggest database of Netdocuments." The usual leader in actually recording the most pages on the Net is the famous AltaVista engine, but often only by a nose.

The third component of any given engine is the search software program. That is what the consumer (the Netsearcher) is using when they type in a keyword. The chief claim made by any engine about their search interface is either that it is the fastest or that it comes up with the most relevant hits, or both.

The search programs are relatively similar in how they search for material, with all of them supporting various advanced query functions that allow for some kind of word linkage. This is done using the increasingly well-known Boolean (named for library scientist Charles Boole) operators, which are connector words such as AND, OR, and NOT that help to refine or narrow a search. Some sites allow for this same Boolean search strategy using plus and minus signs.

So remember, when you search with an Internet search engine, you are using search software designed by the creators of that particular engine to look through an indexed database of Net documents, which in turn was indexed by a spider program. And remember, sometimes a search is only as good or as accurate as the searcher.

Start Your Engines: Finding That Needle in a Haystack

In many ways, search engines *are* the Net. Where would Netusers be without the facility of these mechanically named devices? Somewhat lost, we think.

Unlike a library card catalog (now usually CD-ROM–based), the engines don't have succinct citations of reference by author or topic. Instead they literally index every word of a Net document—which is what make engines both such powerful tools and such blunt instruments—so that when users search for a topic or other item, they are liable to get quite a bit else. This is because, when you put in, for example, the key word "Trees" or "trees" as a search term, you will get not only hits related to things arboreal or suburban, but also, perhaps, the home page of the "Trees" family in Iowa, or the "Flaming Trees" musical group, and so on.

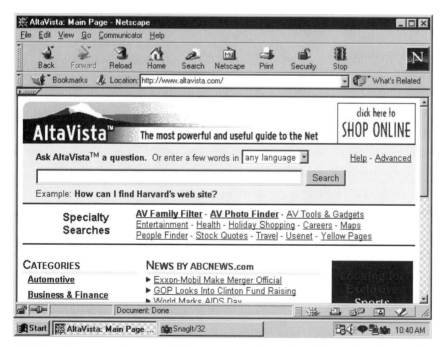

AltaVista lives up to its motto: "The most powerful and useful guide to the Net."

AltaVista *www.altavista.digital.com/*

AltaVista usually leads the pack in having the most exhaustive database of Internet documents and for having the quickest searching programs. This doesn't mean one should use this engine exclusively, but that it should be a top choice when searching.

It should be noted that AltaVista is case sensitive, in that when using a keyword such as "Trees," you will get hits for things treelike, but only in the upper case. But in the reverse, if you put in "trees," you will get tree-related topics in the lower case *and* the upper case.

Another example of how to refine your search is to use a phrase or string of words that is delimited by quotes, such as "Black Entertainment Television." If you typed this without the quotes, your search would result in the engine finding not only the company Black Entertainment Television, but also the occurrence of the words "Black" or "Entertainment" or "Television" anywhere within the Web documents that the engine searches through.

With AltaVista, one can also set a time frame for searches, wherein you might instruct the engine to search for material related to "Black Entertainment Television" between the dates of 15/March/98 and 15/June/98. Then the engine will only retrieve more current material instead of every Web or Net document related to the topic that has been published since the mid-nineties.

Also, in the advanced query mode, one can use a wild card function that requires the placement of an asterisk (*) as a prefix or suffix to any word or words to expand a search. For example, in researching this book about Internet researching and researchers, I could type in the keywords "Internet research*" with the asterisk allowing the engine to also pick up occurrences of the word "researchers" as well.

Another interesting facet of AltaVista searching is a graphical interface that links a group of related topics in chart form to enable you to look for further information on any particular topic. This graphic form of displaying search results may well be the wave of the future, in what is starting to go by the name of "Datamining."

For more on some of the advanced search functions of AltaVista, click on the "Advanced Query" button, and then click the "Help" tutorial.

HotBot *www.hotbot.com/*

The result of a computer project for parallel processing, this engine has become famous as the house engine of *Wired* magazine, which released HotBot for use in 1996 in joint venture with the Inktomi Corporation.

One of the most sophisticated of the search engines, HotBot not only supports the use of keywords and Boolean operands that is standard in all the engines, but also allows one to search by type of file, such as .jpg or .gif (for pictures) or .dbf (for database files). Known as "media" searching, this is a very useful function that allows one to significantly narrow down searches based on the medium of the material that you may be looking for.

Related to the above is the function of searching for material within a particular Internet domain, such as telling HotBot that you're looking for material published within the domain of IBM.com. There is also a date delimiter, so one can specify the time frame of published material that is sought. These, plus a host of other filtering and advanced query functions, make HotBot one of the top engines, earning it "Editors Choice" kudos from *PC Magazine.*

While the Internet Newsroom considers HotBot to be the top power-searching engine, concurring with *PC Magazine,* we would also like to point out that its interface can prove daunting, and you may be some time in setting up your power search parameters, when a simple search with a blunter but more comprehensive engine, such as AltaVista, would serve better.

But then, why not try both?

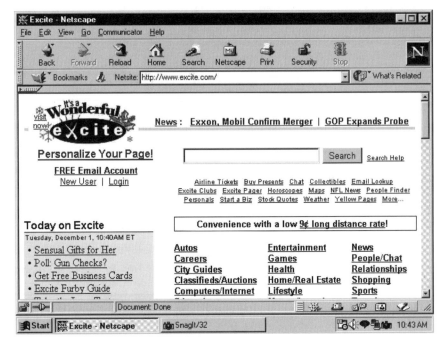

Excite can do natural language searching.

Excite *http://excite.com*

Started by a group of Stanford University students in the early nineties, the Excite search engine has grown to become one of the most used and useful engines on the Net.

Excite's search capabilities include not only the World Wide Web, but also Usenet newsgroups, and Excite has categorized various Internet sites in a topical directory to help information searchers in narrowing down their information search. Like AltaVista, the Excite engine is case sensitive and will search for keywords according to whether you have capitalized them or not. And Excite supports the use of such Boolean operators as AND, OR, and NOT.

Also, Excite will support uses of the + or – signs in order to purposely link or unlink words, e.g., "Bill Clinton – Hillary" or, on the other hand, "Bill Clinton + Hillary," in order to refine one's search. And one can use double quotes to delimit the exact string of words that you are looking for, e.g., "Ford Motor Cars" in order to find exact occurrences of that phrase and not just "Ford" or "Motor" or "Cars," which, as you can imagine, would be highly ineffective.

In what can prove a highly useful facility, Excite allows for natural language searching—also called concept or phrase searching—wherein one can use a concept such as "better living through healthier eating" in order to find relevant information. For more information on any of these more sophisticated search techniques, simply hit the "advanced query" button of Excite or the "Help" button.

Other not-to-be-ignored facets of Excite include its City.Net section, which allows for searching for city information only.

Infoseek *www.infoseek.com/*

The Infoseek engine is similar to the Excite and Lycos engines in that it includes a topical directory in addition to having a large indexed database through which one can do keyword searches. And it has a very useful company directory to facilitate the lookup of business information.

For sophisticated searchers, instead of using such Boolean operators as AND, OR, NOT, and NEAR, the Infoseek interface requires that one use the equally intuitive + and – signs in order to narrow down the search. For example, if you want to find information on Bill Gates, but only in reference to the Microsoft corporation, then you would want to enter "Bill Gates + Microsoft" to ensure that the engine will also look for occurrences of the word Microsoft within the Net documents that it searches.

In order to instruct the engine that you want the occurrence of the word Microsoft to appear in close reference to Bill Gates, instead of the Boolean operand NEAR, one uses square brackets around the whole string of words—i.e., [Bill Gates + Microsoft]—which will look for the word "Microsoft" within one hundred words of "Bill Gates."

While the Infoseek engine will, by default, interpret the word AND between strings of words, if you want to be certain it catches a name such as Bill Gates as such, you should use double quotes around that

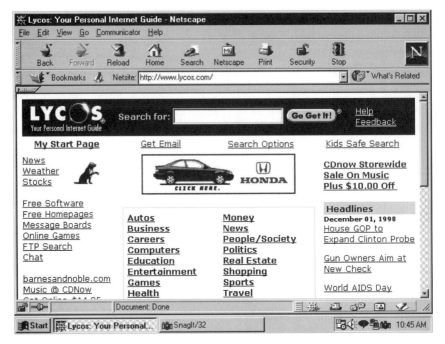

Lycos is one of the original search engines and is still a top contender.

name (i.e., "Bill Gates") or any other string of words that must be found together in your search.

Like AltaVista, the InfoSeek engine is case sensitive, so one will want to capitalize or not, depending on whether one wants to find proper names or common nouns. Infoseek also provides many customizations such as e-mail news delivery, a customized financial portfolio, and foreign language searching.

Lycos *http://lycos.com*

This aptly named engine (its name means "wolf spider" in Latin) is one of the granddaddies of the search engines and is still one of the tops, with a large database and quick searches.

Since its original conception at Carnegie Mellon University in 1994, this engine has become markedly more sophisticated. Presently, some

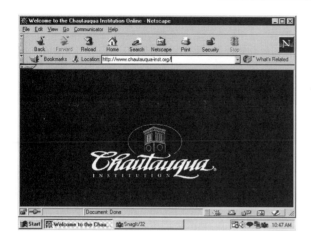

The Chautauqua Institution Web site is just one example of what you can find on the Net using search engines.

of its offerings include a topical directory section, a City Guide information directory, peoplefinders, and such useful partnerships as that with the Dun and Bradstreet business guide to facilitate finding company information. Also, there are the Lycos Point reviews, which give editorial rating under a top 5 percent category to the most useful information sites on the Internet.

Lycos searches the World Wide Web (but not the Usenet) and also has a Pictures and Sound lookup category for specifically finding graphical or audio material. The various search techniques allowable on Lycos are comparable to many of the other engines, such as using double quotes (" ") to delimit a set of words or a phrase that you want to look for exactly, and the use of + and – signs to include must-have words or exclude must-not-have words. There are also pull-down menus that allow you to customize a search such that strings of keywords will have a "high, medium, or low" match.

A Search Engine Come Lately: Northern Light

Launched during the summer of 1997, the Northern Light search engine at *www.nlsearch.com* or *www.northernlight.com* is a relatively new kid on the block, but has already garnered many favorable, if not rave reviews, from Netexperts.

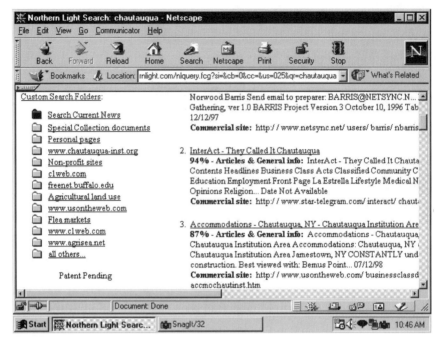

The Northern Light engine creates topical folders for you.

With many facets derived from the world of library science, Northern Light has not only a large indexed database of Web sites and other Net resources, but also boasts a "special collection" of full-text articles. The latter database holds nearly two thousand proprietary sources, including magazines, journals, books, and newswires.

When searching, an information hunter can search either the Net index or the proprietary database, individually or simultaneously. Users should note that in the case of special collection holdings, there is a fee that ranges from $1 to $4 for articles, although for subscribers, there is a provision whereby the first fifty downloads are free. Also, there is a hassle-free, money-back guarantee for downloads that proved irrelevant.

The searching syntax is the same as that found in most other search engines, with the + sign meaning that any two given keywords must be linked, and the use of OR and NOT acting to separate words or eliminate a word altogether, as in "Rock + Roll NOT The Strawberry Alarm Clock."

One of the particularly useful, and also distinguishing, characteristics of the NL engines are the "custom folders" that appear adjacent to the listing of your search results. The folders contain the same information, but sorted by subject (e.g., animal, vegetable, mineral), type of information (e.g., press release, product review, maps), and also by information source (e.g., educational, governmental, or other types of Web sites).

And often these folders hold "subfolders" that break down the information even further. As an example of this, the Internet Newsroom searched for information on the famous "Chautauqua" movement, which still continues on in various places as a cultural, artistic, and literary educational force, and the following folders were developed by the NL engine. (*See graphic on previous page.*)

While the millions of indexed Web sites compiled by Northern Lights puts it closely in competition with such engines as AltaVista, HotBot, Infoseek, or Lycos, it is the construction of its folders that helps to separate it from the pack. For instance, the "subject" folder category uses a hierarchy of over 200,000 subject terms that were formulated by Northern Lights' staff of librarians. This type of cross-referencing against the indexed database of Web sites helps to markedly order (compared with other engines) the information you may be searching for.

It could be that the Northern Lights engine is a real harbinger of things to come as it takes some tentative steps toward searching that is more intuitive.

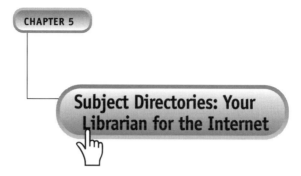

CHAPTER 5

Subject Directories: Your Librarian for the Internet

The Internet has become a vast archive of information, but its usefulness as an information resource is dependent not only on search engines, but also on subject directories that help to bring organization to the maelstrom of information the exists on the Net. Here, we take a look at two top directory spots on the Net, starting with the famous Yahoo service.

Yahoo *www.yahoo.com*

The premier and most popular of this type of directory is the Yahoo subject guide. Yahoo had modest beginnings in the early nineties as a project to catalog the Net by two Stanford University electrical engineering doctoral students, Jerry Yang and David Filo. The whimsical name of Yahoo was not only a reference to *Gulliver's Travels*, but as an acronym that stands for "yet another hierarchical officious oracle," referring in jest to the many different projects started during that era in Net history that were attempting to bring some order to the Net.

Yahoo was an immediate success with the then-much-smaller Net community, and this list of links quickly went private with the help of some small investment capital, after having been hosted on a school

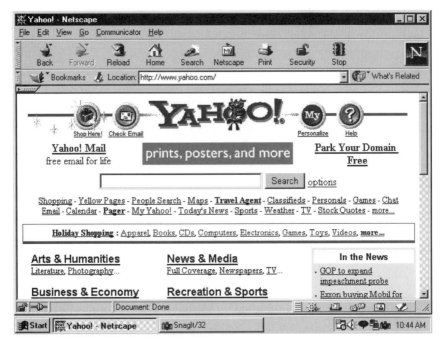

Yahoo is probably the most visited Web site on the Net for information and other assistance.

computer server. As we approach the turn of the century, Yahoo has grown markedly to encompass not only the main Yahoo, but individual country Yahoos that range from Yahoo UK, Yahoo France, and Yahoo Deutschland to Yahoo Korea and Yahoo Japan.

Now a public corporation, the formerly little Yahoo is valued on the stock market at over a billion dollars. And needless to say, Yang and Filo have suspended their doctoral studies for the time being. With an estimate of nearly 100 million page views a day on the Yahoo global network, the number of persons using Yahoo as an information resource roughly translates to a lot!

The term "hierarchical directory" simple means that in the Yahoo and similar directories, the subject categories go from general to specific, as in a researcher first starting with the subject of "computers" and then narrowing his or her research to something more specific, such as "Dell" computers. Another example would be a subject hierarchy such as "rec-reation/hobbies/model airplanes."

In comparison to search engines, Yahoo and similar directories help the Net researcher to get more specific information more easily and quickly. Yahoo librarian Anne Callery wrote about this difference in a paper delivered during a librarian conference that focused on using the Net. In her paper, Callery praised the greater relevance of "hits" using a Net directory vs. search engines.

"There are several advantages to searching a hierarchical subject," Callery wrote. "Higher relevancy rate of items retrieved, less false hits. For example, try running a search (using a search engine) for informa-tion about surfing. In order to find the sites about riding a board on the waves, you'll have to wade through an awful lot of sites."

She also cites a related advantage: not having to use Boolean opera-tors in order to narrow one's topic of research, as one would with search engines. "For example, if a user wants to find sites for organizations in the field of physics, she doesn't have to search for 'physics + organiza-tions *or* societies *or* associations,' etc. She looks under the category 'physics' (on a subject directory, such as Yahoo) browses a short list of subcategories, selects a subcategory called 'organizations,' and there are the sites (that the researcher was looking for). It's not necessary for the user to bring these entities together herself; they are already ar-ranged that way."

The main directory page of Yahoo has fourteen chief categories, in-cluding Arts and Humanities, Business and Economy, Computers and Internet, Education, Entertainment, Government, Health, News and Media, Recreation and Sports, Reference, Regional, Science, Social Sci-ence, and Society and Culture. And, of course, there are subsequently hundreds of thousands of subcategories that ultimately stem from these key main categories. For instance, the first three subcategories listed for Reference are Libraries, Dictionaries, Quotations, or from Regional, there are the initial subcategories of Countries, Regions, U.S. States.

In a review of Yahoo the *San Jose Mercury News* noted that "Yahoo is closest in spirit to the work of Linnaeus, the eighteenth century bota-nist whose classification system organized the natural world."

Also included in the Yahoo service are a growing number of Yahoo city guides, My Yahoo (a personalization service), Yahoo Mail, Pager (for online instant messaging), Chats, Message Boards, Stock Portfolios, Yahoo Classifieds, and Yahoo Games. There is also a children's and young adult section called Yahooligans, and a Yahoo for seniors.

Encyclopædia Britannica Internet Directory *www.ebig.com*

The venerable *Encyclopædia Britannica* (EB) has created the Britannica Internet Directory, where the encyclopedic editors of the *Britannica* use their razor-sharp skills to cut through the chaff of the Net. In Netsurfing terms, this is known as the "human filter," which doesn't rely on preprogrammed search engine spiders and keyword databases, but instead actually categorizes Web sites by hand. This filtering is, in part, much like that of the famous Yahoo directory, but with an even more exclusive and discriminating hand.

Each listed Web site has been "chosen, reviewed and rated by *Britannica* editors," said an EB spokeswoman. So far, about 125,000 Web sites have been indexed. According to the company, this selection process, the site reviews, and EB's "search and retrieval" system, which searches through the compiled Web sites, gives the user more relevant findings compared with other Net directories and search engines.

"The Britannica Internet Guide is the first navigation service to make real progress toward the goal of finding reliable information on the Internet," said Peter Meyerhoff, senior editor at *Britannica* and the editorial director of the Guide. "Other services turn up hundreds of irrelevant hits, and there's no way to tell the good sources from the questionable ones. Our editors make it easy for people to quickly locate authoritative and useful information on thousands of topics."

His remarks were echoed by a veteran journalist on the CARR-L Listserv (computer-aided research and reporting) who said, "The *Encyclopædia Britannica*'s Internet guide has become my first choice when I'm using the Net to research a subject. Its big advantage is that it's structured by some of the world's best and most experienced information retrieval professionals."

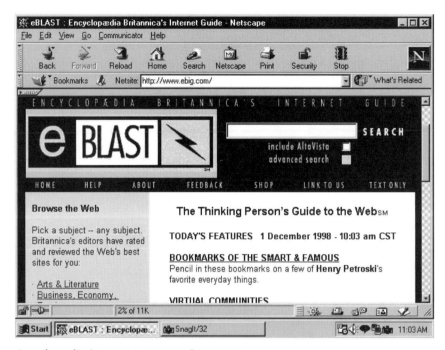

Encyclopædia Britannica Internet Directory

Directory editors evaluate Web sites based on "depth and quality" and use a hard-nosed protocol to judge sites based on the credentials and authority of each Web site's author, frequency of revision, and ease of navigation. Functional and aesthetic judgments are made based on the effective (or ineffective) use of multimedia, and "elegance of design."

The Britannica Directory allows users to search by keyword, name, or phrase, or they can peruse the topical table of contents. This subject outline includes such informational categories as Art and Literature, Health and Medicine, News and Current Events, Science, Technology and Mathematics, and Social Science. There are fourteen categories.

In addition to its new Internet directory, the Britannica has a fee-based service at *www.eb.com/search/* that allows journalists to access most of the contents of its famed encyclopedia for $85 annually. A limited search can be performed free.

CHAPTER 6

Covering the Waterfront: MetaSearch Engines

It's not as if the general class of search engines—AltaVista, Excite, Lycos, etc.—don't turn up enough material as is when used in Net-searching, but for absolutely comprehensive results in one's information hunting, the class of "metasearch" engines should be considered.

What, many readers may ask, are metasearch engines, and why should they be used? The short answer is that the metasearch engines (metaengines) are the search engines of search engines, meaning that they make informational queries to several, if not many, other engines all at once. One example, aptly named "Dogpile" (after the phenomenon in rugby where players all jump on each other), searches through twenty-five different Internet search engines. Other well-known metaengines are SavvySearch and MetaCrawler.

By necessity, these metaengines are more powerful than the average single search engine, but in that same vein, they take more time in their queries because they must go through many other engines. Where they excel over single search engines, such as AltaVista, is that they will oftentimes return answers to relatively obscure queries that a single engine may miss.

Metasearch engines work in the same manner as the standard search engines. The metaengines each have a search entry form where the information searcher can put in the keyword or words that are relevant to what they are looking for. There is a search button adjacent to the keyword form that one clicks to kick off the search. Other more complicated configurations of the metasearch engines allow for setting the date parameters you wish to search within—e. g., 2/15/97 to 5/15/98— and the use of Boolean operators AND, OR, NOT, and the "proximity" operator NEAR. These, of course, are also functions usually allowed by the standard engines.

Dogpile *www.dogpile.com*

The metaengine Dogpile lives up to its name by virtue of the fact that it searches twenty-five different Internet engines, such as the following:

- On the Web, it searches AltaVista, Excite, Lycos, Infoseek, Thunderstone, PlanetSearch, and such guides as Yahoo
- For Usenet searching, it goes through DejaNews, Reference, AltaVista, and what has become known as the DejaNews old database.
- For areas of the Net that have file transfer protocols (FTP downloads) it searches through Filez and FTP search.
- There is a search through the Internet news wire feed, including Yahoo News Headlines, Excite News, and InfoSeek NewsWires.

Dogpile supports the Boolean and proximity operators AND, OR, NOT, and NEAR, allowing users to narrow and refine their multisearches. Keep in mind, however, that all the engines that Dogpile will search for you may not always support such operators. In the case of engines, for instance, that don't support the use of the operator NOT, Dogpile will simply subtract that word from your search syntax. This doesn't quite yield the same results as saying "Bill Clinton NOT Monica Lewinsky," but will help somewhat. Dogpile points out that if you don't use an AND connector, the engine assumes it anyway, such that a search for "Free AND Mac AND Software" is the same as a search for "Free Mac Software." The Dogpile multisearch engine also allows the use of quotes and parentheses.

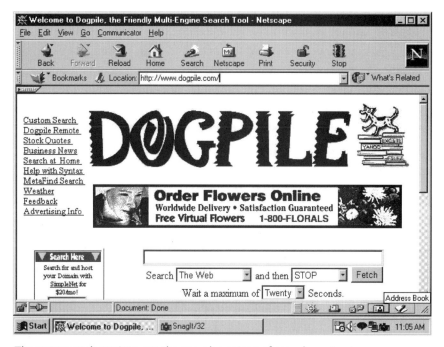

The metasearch engines are the search engines of search engines!

After entering your keyword or words, you press the "Fetch" button next to the keyword form, and "Arfie," as Dogpile calls its searcher software, will go through three engines at a time before returning results. When you finish going through those results, you press the search button at the bottom of the search hits page to search the next set of three engines.

And thus, the "Dogpile" begins to grow and grow.

SavvySearch *http://savvysearch.com*

Founded in 1995 as computer science experiment at Colorado State University, SavvySearch is one of the oldest of the metaengines. As of this writing in 1998, the SavvySearch Web site doesn't support the standard Boolean operators, but it does have a handy feature for narrowing down your searches of other engines by certain categories. After you put in a keyword or words for your search, you also can click a set of topical categories that includes Web Indexes, Software, People, Reference, Usenet News, Technical Reports, and Entertainment.

Once you designate a category, the SavvySearch begins its perusal of multiple search engines. For example, if you are looking for background on San Francisco Mayor Willie Brown, you might designate the categories People and Usenet News. The Internet Newsroom and other reviewers of this engine have described this function as a powerful option for searching the Net.

Another search refinement is the Query Options, which take the place, in part, of the Boolean operators that Savvy doesn't support. Using a drop-down menu you can search for documents containing "all query terms" (wherein you tell the engine that you want all keywords to appear in your search); "all query terms as a phrase;" and "any query term." You can also specify how many results you want from each engine—ten, twenty, thirty, forty, or fifty.

Also, the hits from each engine that SavvySearch has explored can be displayed on Brief, Normal, or Verbose format, depending on how much information you may want or need from the citations that are listed. The Normal category will include the author, date, URL of the Net resources, a synopsis (usually just the lead paragraph of that document), and the document title.

And lastly, one can integrate the results that SavvySearch has found to eliminate duplicate citations from different engines that Savvy has probed.

MetaCrawler *www.metacrawler.com*

Started by University of Washington student Erik Selbert as a project for his master's degree in computer science during 1995, this engine is now operated by Go2Net, an Internet company that has helped improve an already well-regarded metasearch engine by giving it more infrastructure and tech support.

The current MetaCrawler has a variety of helpful facets for refining one's search before launching this arachnid-denominated device through the various search engines on the Net. Besides the standard search entry blank for one's keywords, there are also a number of separate buttons that allow you to define searching options and restrict the range of searching.

For the keywords, you can tell MetaCrawler to search the words as a phrase (not just finding the words, but the complete phrase); to search for *all* of the words; or to search for *any* of the words that you type into the search blank. For phrase searching, you use parentheses to enclose the phrase.

Then there are the search restriction buttons. You can narrow the search by region—e.g., only through resources from Europe—or by certain Web sites—e.g., look only through U.S. corporate Web sites—each of which can markedly help with the relevance of one's hits.

The regional restrictions range from Everywhere to North American, Europe, Asia, Australia, South American, Africa, down to searching just through your particular Internet domain. The Web site restriction includes searching Any Company, Organization, Government Web site (US), Military (US), and through International Web sites.

Also, under the left-hand column Resources heading, one can limit his or her searches to the following categories: Career Center, Ultimate Directory, Yellow Pages, People Find, Maps & Direction, Classifieds, Companies Online, City Guides, Weather Forecast, and Travel Store. There is also a handy Marketplace section for shopping online that includes *Outpost.com* (for software), *Priceline.com* (for airline tickets), CarSmart and 1-800-Florals.

Other Metaengines

For purposes of space, I have not reviewed and outlined the details of each multisearch engine. But keep in mind that there are other engines that are just as useful and efficient as the ones written about above. Here is a list of several other well-known and often-used metasearch engines:

- Inference Find (*www.inference.com/ifind/*) Active since May 1995, this metasearch engine has the distinction of not listing its findings simply as a lists of hits. Instead, Inference Find makes "inferences" and arranges finding according to topical subjects. It searches AltaVista, Excite, Lycos, WebCrawler, and Yahoo.

- HuskySearch (*http://huskysearch.cs.washington.edu/*) As an encore to the development of his MetaCrawler, graduate student Erik Selbert launched this new engine in early 1997 at the University of Washington.
- OneSeek (*www.oneseek.com*) One of the newest of the metaengines, OneSeek displays the results of its multisearches (three engines at once) side-by-side.

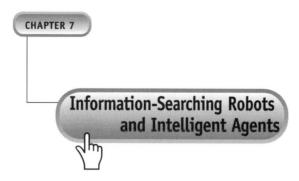

CHAPTER 7

Information-Searching Robots and Intelligent Agents

The principle behind search engines is a simple one—the engines employ spidering technology that travels through Internet documents recording them to the engine's database, which one can then search using keywords. But what if you had your own personal spider for going through the Net that could not only work when you unleash it, but also search while you are doing other tasks, even while you are sleeping?

These spiders that are used by search engines, and by individuals, are also known as "bots," short for "robots." The name is fitting in the sense that robots have always been thought of as machines that do the bidding of their human masters, who simply give them commands and set them loose. In essence, these "cyberbots" have been created to serve as personal research assistants for their respective users.

Bots are actually software programs that can act independently of their human users, once given a delegated function. "Bots are just scripts of information (programs) that go across the Net and do tasks," explains Marcus Zillman, creator of the BotSpot Web site. For a good overview about bots of all kinds, the BotSpot site (*http://botspot.com/*) has a great deal of background information and links to many types of bots.

What Bots Do

According to Zillman, there are three basic types of functions that bots perform—searching, monitoring, and, though still somewhat unsophisticated, the function of evaluating information. Because of advances in artificial intelligence programs, this latter function will begin to appear more frequently shortly after the year 2000, Zillman conjectures.

In part, the value of researching bots is that they can "create mini Yahoos" by compiling links that are highly specific and relevant to the individual user, said Zillman. In general, Zillman notes, the sudden advances in usage of bots by the average Netsurfer have been made possible by "increases in computer power." And though there are no reliable statistics on the number of persons using bots, Zillman points to the nearly 200,000 visitors who sojourn through his Web site each month.

At present, the creators of these bots, and those who use them, frequently point out that research bots are best at doing a specific task—"find me the Gettysburg Address" (and material related to the Gettysburg Address)—vs. a more general task, such as "find things about the Civil War." And in particular, these bots excel at finding nontextual information, such as sound and graphic files, an area where the general search engines are still somewhat weak.

A technology reviewer for *CNet* (a popular technology news Web site and TV program) said the following about this: "Looking to add to your collection of Nirvana MIDI files? Turn a spider loose on a few fan [Web] sites before you go to bed, and odds are you'll wake up with a hard drive full of music."

The various categories of bots include not only searching bots, but also shopping bots, chat (or chatter) bots (they answer questions), and intuitive (evaluative) bots such as FireFly that will build a database of your musical interests based on your previous selections of music.

While chatterbots are starting to become employed in the corporate world as serious working guides to company Web sites, they also have a lighthearted side. Many Netsurfers simply like various chatterbots, such as ShallowRed or Erin the Bartender, for the sole and novel purpose of talking with something that's completely synthetic. "People are fascinated with things that go BOO in the night," said Zillman about some of the novelty of chatterbots. "They [Netsurfers] can't believe they are talking to a computer." He adds, however, that serious or lighthearted, these chatterbots will add greatly to the interactivity of Web sites by helping to guide Netsurfers around.

The Extempo company has created a number of chatterbots, which it calls "Imp Characters" and which have a variety of applications, according to the company Web site. "Imp Characters can play many roles, for example as a spokesperson in an online product showroom, a tour guide on a company Web site, or a bartender in an online pub," Extempo promo materials read. "Interacting through actions, gestures, facial expressions, and conversation, each Imp Character engages and delights users with its distinctive personality and individual style."

Chatterbots are also sometimes called "avatars," from the Hindu concept of how supernatural creatures manifest themselves in the physical world. A tome on the subject of complex bots, the *Agent Sourcebook* (written by Harrison Caglayan, published by Wiley Publishing), addresses the topic of the more sophisticated version of the bot programs that are known as "agents" or "intelligent agents," for the same reason they are termed bots—a dictionary definition of agent is "A person or thing that acts . . . or is empowered to act, for another." You can read more from the *Agent Sourcebook* at *www.opensesame.com/agents/*.

Future expectation (i.e., two to five years) for these intelligent agents is that the technology will be able to act almost independently of their human masters. They will search and make stock trades, or remember to buy and send flowers on the occasion of a wife's or husband's birthday. But before one gets too enamored of these possibilities, let this writer hasten to add that intelligent agents aren't quite that intelligent yet. These agents are closer to the robot stage than to the intuitive servant stage of evolution.

Nevertheless, whether one calls their search-and-find software a bot or an agent, it is useful all the same. Many readers may not even realize that they are already using various forms of bot technology.

THE INTERNET RESEARCH GUIDE

Research Bots

A top bot, as reviewed by the BotSpot, is the BullsEye bot created by the Intelliseek company (*www.intelliseek.com/*). BullsEye employs several intelligent agent programs in order to tap into over three hundred search engines and six hundred plus databases on the Net. It functions not only by finding information, but also by analyzing, filtering, managing, and tracking various data relevant to any given user.

The infoGIST company has created a number of Web searching bots, which the company calls infoFinders. These include a PR infoFinder, Web infoFinder, and Career infoFinder. They all can be downloaded from the company Web site at *www.infogist.com/*.

Autonomy Agentware (*www.agentware.com/*) provides the search agent software for a number of new media publishers, including News Corp, which helps to personalize these Web sites. Other search bots include CyBot (*www.theartmachine.com/cybot.htm*) and the Web Bandit (*www.jwsg.com/webbandit.htm*).

Many news Web sites have forms of bots that will tailor their news clipping to the individual taste of any information consumer. One of the earliest, and still one of the most useful, of the robot-personalized clipping services is the NewsHound, hosted by the *San Jose Mercury News* at *www.newshound.com/main.htm*. Another well-regarded clipping bot is *Wired* magazine's NewBot, at the HotWired Web site *www.wired.com/newbot/*.

Chatterbots

A comprehensive rundown of chatterbots (also called "interactive characters" and "avatars") can be found at the BotSpot (*www.chatterbots.com/*). ShallowRed, created by Neurostudio Inc., has a variety of avatar bots for use as Web site tour guides at *http://isis.neurostudio.com/*.

The NetSage company (*www.netsage.com/*) has a number of chatterbots for sale, particularly for use in the education market (thus the name "sage" for their bots). The Extempo company, inventor of the oft-cited

Erin-the-Bartender chatterbot, has created a number of interactive characters called Imps that have applications in e-commerce, entertainment, and corporate communications. Imp Characters can be found at *www. extempo.com.*

Shopping Bots

Shopping bots don't really shop for the user, but rather they engage in price comparisons (e.g., find me a Smashing Pumpkins CD for less the $10) and then report back with a list of likely Web sites carrying the item you requested. Among the shopping bots are Junglee (*www. junglee.com*), which shops for electronics, music, books, and clothing; Jango (*www.jango.com*), which shops for electronics, sports equipment, and even groceries; and Travelocity (*www.travelocity.com*), which shops travel costs. One of the biggies in terms of popularity and public familiarity, the Travelocity Web site features bot technology that helps you find the lowest airfare to any given destination.

CHAPTER 8

"Good Luck, Mr. Gorsky!"

The following is a case study in judging the veracity of some information that you will come across on the Internet. There is a category of information that began to become known as "urban legends" some years ago—e.g., the cat in the microwave, human organ thieves, etc.—and these perennial legends, and many new ones, have found their way onto the Internet, where they have gone into overdrive.

This example regards a story that has been actively circulating for several years on Internet newsgroups and through chain e-mail, about astronaut Neil Armstrong and what he is purported to have said as he set foot upon the moon.

"Good luck, Mr. Gorsky," Armstrong is alleged to have cryptically said.

What Did Neil Armstrong Really Say on the Moon?

From corporate offices to scientific research labs, and no doubt through many academic computer servers, there has been e-mail received—passed on by friends and such—which contains the account of a latter-day speech by astronaut Neil Armstrong to a group in Tampa Bay. According to the account, Armstrong was delivering a speech before a group in Tampa Bay, Florida, when he was asked about why he said, "Good luck, Mr. Gorsky," during his moon mission. The account that has been circulating about this speech cites the fact that Armstrong has been asked this question before, but he always declined to answer it. This time, however, he gave a long-awaited explanation.

Armstrong said that, at long last, he could freely answer this question because the "Mr. Gorsky" in question was dead. It seems that when Armstrong was a boy, his family lived next to a family named Gorsky. One day, while playing ball with his brother in the back yard, Armstrong found himself chasing a pop fly into the neighbors' back yard, where it landed right outside the Gorskys' bedroom window. Hearing raised voices as he was retrieving the ball, young Armstrong stopped for a moment to listen. He overheard Mrs. Gorsky shrieking at her husband, "Oral sex? Oral sex you want! You'll get oral sex when the kid next door walks on the moon!"

And the rest is history. Or is it?

According to NASA spokesman Brian Welch, a review of transcripts from Armstrong's *Apollo 11* mission contains no reference of any kind to "Mr. Gorsky." Other knowledgeable sources also dispute the truth of this story. But because of the effective global dissemination of this tale via the Internet, it has been "dependably" passed around and around as the truth, with little to stop it in lieu of someone sending mass e-mail unmasking the story as erroneous. Also, because the Internet passes material along in print (versus stories told at the office water cooler), the stories have the credibility that often accrues to printed matter.

"With the Internet, there's an enormous amount of information that hasn't been filtered through anything," said a scientist familiar with the Net in a recent news interview. "It didn't have to find a publisher, it didn't have to go through peer review to become available to an enormous amount of people."

The "Good luck, Mr. Gorsky" comment attributed to Armstrong has become what's known as a "Netmyth." And because these Netmyths can be massively duplicated word-for-word via e-mail and other means, this begs the question of how to judge information.

One good rule of thumb is the old "consider the source" rule. While there is much "unfiltered" information on the Net that hasn't been vetted by news organizations or any scholarly journals as being accurate, the majority of the information available via the Net is from credible sources. If you read information straight from the NASA Web site (*www.nasa.gov*), for instance, you can safely say that that material carries with it the credibility of that organization. Here, for instance, is part of a strange-but-true press release from NASA'S Goddard Space Flight Center about a "space disturbance" detected in fall of 1995:

SPACE DISTURBANCE DETECTED BY NASA SATELLITE
BEFORE REACHING EARTH

A NASA spacecraft detected a huge interplanetary disturbance which struck the Earth's protective magnetic field on Oct. 18, producing a magnetic storm and auroral displays, or "Northern Lights," that persisted for two days.

The phenomenon was visible in the United States as far south as Denver, according to scientists at NASA's Goddard Space Flight Center, Greenbelt, Md., who reported critical satellite data to other government agencies and scientists around the world.

—Found at: *ftp://pao.gsfc.nasa.gov/pub/PAO/releases/1995/95-202.txt*

The credibility that you grant NASA stands true of government Web sites as well. Also, the myriad of well-known newspapers and magazines that are now publishing on the Internet carry with them the credibility of those organizations. And official university sites can be relied upon for research and other scholarly information.

But in this same vein, one must watch out for what they may find through a university student's *personal* Web page, as scholarly as it may seem. One must also bring the skepticism one would normally bring to propaganda when looking through the home pages of political candidates or parties. And researchers must particularly be on guard when viewing the Internet material of fringe groups or other organizations with an ax to grind.

SECTION II

Business Research on the Net

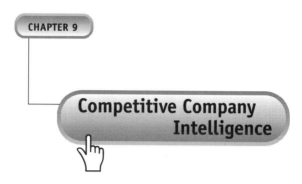

CHAPTER 9

Competitive Company Intelligence

"Many people don't realize just how much you can learn about your rivals by accessing the Internet," said Leonard M. Fuld, in an interview with the *New York Times* about competitive business research on the Net. "From prospective clients to product specs, it's out there. And we are not talking about some secret Web site that you need to access."

According to Fuld, who owns Fuld and Company, a competitive intelligence (CI) consulting firm, there is much about a company that can be learned by looking at such public information on the Net as organization charts, customer lists, and executive biographies. And often, company Web sites may have information about business strategies or planned product releases that may prove highly useful to competitors, Fuld and other similar competitive intelligence experts say.

One can also learn about competitors by looking at their online job postings to see who they may be hiring, by collating all the online news service reports about a particular corporation, and by trolling through newsgroup discussion forums where company employees or company critics may be discussing company affairs. While much of this type of information has been available years before the Net—such as in company annual reports—the Internet has increased the speed of access to this type of competitive intelligence such that one can get the information quickly and from many different sources.

Nevertheless, Fuld and other experts caution that while much useful information awaits a corporate sleuth online, one still has to sift through and analyze that information. "Of course the Internet is a tool, and not an answer machine," Fuld told the *New York Times*. "So you need to be really patient and able to dig deep." He says that by looking at such things as company hiring patterns, one can get an idea of business areas where a company is placing increased emphasis.

In talking about Net research to *FastCompany* magazine, Fuld cited the example of finding a feature article in a local newspaper that provided telling details about the CEO of a certain company, such as "this guy took a bus to [a] nearby town to visit one of the company's plants. Those few words were a small but important sign to me that this company was going to be incredibly cost-conscious."

"The more articles that you collect, the more bios that you download, the better you can get at creating these (management) profiles. All this material is on the Web," Fuld told *FastCompany*.

With regard to the CEO who liked to take buses, Fuld also cited the example of a local article on life "at one of his (the CEO) company's factories, complete with great stuff on how many people worked there, what the average salary was—remarkable stuff. We put that information together with other data and developed a pretty reliable estimate of manufacturing cost at this plant."

Voilà!

The Fuld and Company Web site (*www.fuld.com*) is a topnotch spot for starting your CI search on various companies, with links to over 300 business-related Web sites and research resources. Also, the Fuld site provides some useful tutorials on the basics of competitive intelligence. You can also try the Society of Competitive Intelligence Professionals at *www.scip.org*.

For researching high-tech companies and their executives, the CorpTech Web site (*www.corptech.com*) provides information on 45,000 companies and over 170,000 executives.

To see who is hiring and what kind of persons they are looking for (or if you're looking for a position yourself) there are a number of employment hunting locales on the Net such as the Monster Board (*www. monsterboard.com*) and CareerPath.Com (*www.careerpath.com/*).

To research product information, you should go to the IBM Patent Server (*www.patents.ibm.com/*). This database, maintained by IBM, has two million patents archived online.

Net Scuttlebut (What People Are Saying)

The premier search engine for picking up Internet-based discussions is DejaNews (*www.dejanews.com*), which tracks the various newsgroups (topical discussion groups) and is searchable by topic, company name, product, or indeed, any type of keyword.

News Searching

Excite NewsTracker *(http://nt.excite.com)* is updated several times a day, collecting thousands of articles from over 300 Web newspapers and magazines. NewsTracker has a search function that allows you to use keywords to retrieve articles from its news index. It also provides a custom news clipping service.

American Journalism Review's Newslink (*http://ajr.newslink.org*) links to more than 3,500 online newspapers the world over. Editor and Publisher (*www.mediainfo.com/*) also has links to online newspapers around the world.

Databases

DialogWeb (*www.dialogweb.com*) searches 450 databases and lists findings, but requires a fee for downloads.

CHAPTER 10

Financial Research for the Individual Investor

Will the financial markets continue their roller coaster behavior as we approach the twenty-first century? Nobody knows the answer to that question. But ordinary investors today have a formidable resource to track the market that was not widely available during that market collapse a decade ago. The Internet is loaded with investment information, and also makes online investment easy.

The volume of market statistics and news that is available via the Net continues to grow and become more solid. This information ranges from Security and Exchange Commission documents to constantly updated stock quotes, statistical databases, financial magazines, and newsletters. There are also numerous actual trading Web sites. And most of this information is free.

Boom or Bust? Riding the Stock Market Roller Coaster Online

One of the top spots for gathering market information is the Securities and Exchange Commission's EDGAR Net site (*www.sec.gov*). EDGAR (electronic data gathering and retrieval) is an online database whose basic offerings are the standard corporate financial filings, such as 10Ks (annual reports), that companies must file with the SEC. They give you a

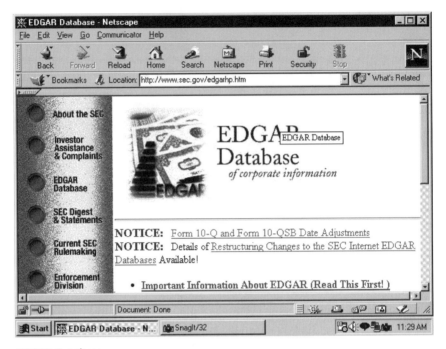

EDGAR Database

rundown of any particular company's financial health. Recently EDGAR also began providing breakdowns of corporate filings that are far simpler to use and analyze and can include things like the amount of executive compensation, or graphs of a company's performance.

Another good stopping point run by Uncle Sam is the Web site for the Federal Reserve Board of the United States and each of the eleven regional Federal Reserve Banks. There is a variety of financial and statistical information at these locations, as well as economic outlook reports that are filed periodically. To peruse the Fed, start at the site of the Federal Reserve Board in Washington, which has links to each of the eleven regional banks. The address is *www.bog.frb.fed.us/*.

The *Wall Street Journal*, that giant of financial reporting, went online more than a year ago (*www.wsj.com*). Initially, it was a free site, but now there is a modest fee, and the information offerings here are sufficiently worthwhile that the *Journal* Interactive is worth the subscription cost.

Featured, of course, is global news of companies and markets, updated on a continual basis. There also is an archive of past articles.

Of even greater interest to those seeking market and financial information is the "Briefing Book" on thousands of companies that the *Journal* has prepared. And there is also continuously updated stock quote information that comes through with just a slight delay.

Also top-of-the-charts, so to speak, for financial news reporting is the new CNNFN Web site (*http://cnnfn.com/markets/quotes.html*) which, like the *Journal,* offers frequently updated business news and market coverage. Also similar to the *Journal,* CNNFN offers access to stock quotes, delayed by fifteen minutes from their actual release. One key point about CNNFN is that it is free.

In terms of just getting data "straight from the market's mouth," there are a number of locales on the World Wide Web that have nothing but market quotes. One of the best known is PCQuote (*www.pcquote.com/*), which boasts that it is the "world's leading provider of online stock

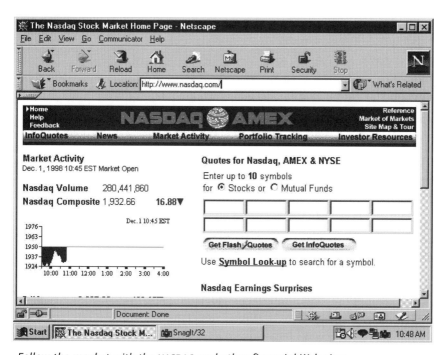

Follow the market with the NASDAQ *and other financial Web sites.*

quotes." Its free offerings include multi-quote format or symbol lookup services of stock prices that it issues with a slight time delay. For subscribing members, real-time quotes are available.

Another Web service that features quotes is the StockMaster site (*www.stockmaster.com*), which allows you to look up the price on stocks by name.

As mentioned in chapter 2, all of the stock exchanges are now on the Net, including the American Stock Exchange (*www.amex.com*), the NASDAQ (*www.nasdaq.com/*), and the New York Stock Exchange (*www. nyse.com*).

Most market observers agree that one of the major market trends of the last several years has been the increasing movement of money into mutual funds. The explosion of 401(k) retirement programs, which supplanted conventional pension plans, is largely responsible for billions of dollars being dumped into mutual funds by workers. The move toward mutual funds has been closely followed by an increase in the amount of mutual fund information that is on the Net. The Investment Company Institute (*www.ici.com*) is a good place to obtain an overview of mutual funds.

If you prefer to start with something simple and written in plain English (only a modicum of "marketese"), you might want to click through the pages of the online version of *Mutual Funds* magazine (*www.mfmag.com*). The mutual fund database that is accessible at this site has information on approximately six thousand funds. There are several levels of access, including Guest, Registered User, and Charter Members. The latter, as one would imagine, are granted unlimited access to the material gathered by the magazine.

The Networth Information Center, hosted by Quicken.com (*www. quicken.com*), is rated as one of the most popular Web sites dealing with funds. Part of its big draw is its database of seven thousand funds, hosted by the well-known Morningstar group.

The Mutual Fund Café (*www.mfcafe.com*) is primarily aimed at professionals in the fund field, but it is, nevertheless, open to all. Some of the information here includes trend data on the sales of mutual funds, lists of recent fund mergers, and data on publicly traded fund companies. Also try the Money Café at *www.moneycafe.com/moneycafe/stocfund.htm.*

Many investment firms have staked out territory on the Net with their home pages. These include the nation's largest stock broker, Merrill Lynch (*www.ml.com*), and Fidelity, the largest family of mutual funds (*www.fid-inv.com*). Other large firms include Rowe Price (*http://troweprice.com*), Charles Schwab (*www.schwab.com*), and Smith Barney (*www.smithbarney.com*).

While the Net pages are obviously intended to serve as electronic storefronts, they often have some very useful resources. These can include such items as company prospectuses, and performance information on the various funds that each of these firms manage. There is also good background information at these sites for the market novice, including glossaries of financial terms and other similar resources.

CHAPTER 11

More About the EDGARS

O f the many business information services available via the Net, one of the most useful—if not the most useful—is the EDGAR (electronic data gathering analysis and retrieval) system that is maintained by the Securities and Exchange Commission (SEC), but available through several different Web sites.

EDGAR Can Find the Company Information You Need

By way of brief history, the SEC was founded in 1933 to help protect investors from the kind of financial market fraud and excess that resulted in the great 1928 stock market crash. The regulation of the agency has served relatively well since that time to control financial reporting practices by publicly held corporations, and to help inform the public of how these companies perform financially.

Among the reports that public companies must file with the SEC are the following:

- 10K (A comprehensive annual report that includes financial statement audited by outside accountants)
- 10Q (A quarterly report)

- 8K (A required filing for anything considered "materially signifi-cant" for a company)
- Proxy Statement (A version of the annual report that is filed for shareholders)
- Other (Stock registration statements; documents from such indus-tries as mutual funds, insurance companies, broker-dealers, and real estate investment companies)

Any reporter (or other type of researcher) over the age of thirty can remember that the SEC, based in Washington, D.C., housed all the above documents in hard copy or microfiche form. One could spend the day in a document room looking for company financial information. Once one found what one was looking for on the microfiche, for instance, they could then print it out, page by page, in order to get copies.

Then in the mid-eighties, the SEC began work on the EDGAR system, which, until the advent of the World Wide Web, was difficult to use and not widely available via most computer systems. With the common advent of the Net, however, EDGAR has become broadly accessible through not only the SEC, but also through several information com-panies that have packaged the database in an easy-to-use interface.

The best of the available interfaces is the EDGAR Online service cre-ated by Cybernet Data Systems (*www.edgar-online/*). The majority of this service is free, but the up-to-the-minute daily filings with the SEC cost a nominal charge to access; this is how the company makes its money. For reporters and researchers who need information that is timely, the latter is worth the small charge. By contrast, at the actual SEC Web site itself—which is completely free—there is lag in informa-tion so that you won't get that day's filings.

At CyberNet Data's EDGAR Online, the search mechanism is such that one can easily search by using a company name, its stock ticker sym-bol, or even look for information on company executives or CEOs by using that person's name. Probably the most handy function of this version of EDGAR is a search that allows you to break down financial filings by state or city, e.g., telling the search function to find which Il-linois or Chicago companies have just filed their records. In the Internet

Newsroom's opinion, this function is a must for regional reporters and researchers.

EDGAR Online can also send you e-mail notices when certain filings take, such as a notice of something "materially important" that a company didn't necessarily also announce in a press release. To use this service, go to the "WatchList" section. The cost to journalists and students for EDGAR Online is $14.95 per quarter.

The SEC Web site (*www.sec.gov/edgarhp.htm*), which is free, supplies virtually the same information as EDGAR online, with the important caveat that the interface is clunky and ultimately not as useful. For instance, the information is not searchable in the same way, such as by state. Also, for those who want immediate information there is a delay of twenty-four hours on most filings. Still, the SEC EDGAR site is useful and requires no fee or registration.

Finally, the peoplefinder service WhoWhere (*www.whowhere.com/ edgar/index.html*) has expanded to include business information searches using EDGAR as its source.

CHAPTER 12

Need a Mortgage?

The real estate market for homes is exploding this spring, and so is information on the Internet about buying and financing a house. Instead of making a dozen calls to various local mortgage lenders to find out about rates and lending terms, a prospective home buyer (or journalist working on a mortgage story) simply has to fire up his computer and do some Netsurfing.

For example, we asked the WebCrawler search engine to find sites containing the word "mortgage," and it came up with 6,594 hits. Many were local realtor Web sites, but there were numerous mortgage lenders eager to finance homes for buyers.

A good place to get the big picture about current mortgage rates is a site hosted by Mortgage Market Information Services, an independent company which gathers information nationwide about interest rates and points being charged by mortgage lenders and disseminates it via print and the Internet. The address of the site is *www.interest.com/rates.html.*

At that location, there's a clickable U.S. map, which you can use to obtain the latest mortgage rate data for any state. There is also a list of other sections on the site, including information on mortgage trends, a mortgage calculator, city mortgage guides, informative sites for consumers, a discussion group, and an excellent library. The library has a guide on refinancing, a bookshelf of mortgage booklets, a place for first-time mortgage borrowers, and a list of links to other financial sites on the Web.

Fannie Mae, the huge quasi-government operation which buys and sells mortgage instruments, has a Web site called "Home Path," designed to answer consumer questions about mortgages, at *www.homepath. com/*. It includes a rundown on mortgage counselors in local areas, a list of local mortgage lenders, and several home buying guides for consumers. The site has three main divisions: Home Starter for first-time borrowers, Home Purchase for those ready to buy, and Home Refinance for those hunting for a better mortgage.

Another place to obtain an overview is the Web site of the Mortgage Bankers of America (*www.mbaa.org/*), a Washington-based trade association. Most of their information is aimed at mortgage lenders, but there is a section just for consumers. The weekly survey of mortgage applications showed just how explosive today's residential real estate market is. For example, in mid-April, weekly mortgage applications were running 122 percent higher than during a comparable period the previous year.

Robert O'Toole, a vice president of the trade group, stressed in an interview that the volume of mortgage business on the Internet is still small (less than one percent of the $789 billion mortgage business). I visited the Web sites of two large mortgage lenders who do business nationwide: Countrywide (*www.countrywide.com/chl_home/chlframe. html*) and Inland Mortgage (*www.inlandmortgage.com/*). At both sites, you can get current rate information on home loans, as well as actually apply for a loan.

It is also easy to contact local area mortgage lenders on the Internet. I asked a search engine to find "Maryland Mortgage Lenders" and got numerous hits. One was from a mortgage firm in the Maryland suburbs of Washington, D.C., which is where our office is located. Another was for several Maryland branches of the giant Chase Bank of New York. There was also a catch-all site called "Maryland Mortgage Online," which represented a number of mortgage lenders in the state.

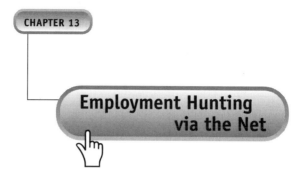

CHAPTER 13

Employment Hunting via the Net

Another way that the Net is changing the world is in the field of good old-fashioned job hunting—not just looking for short-term assignments and contracts—but actually looking for positions of employment.

The Web has quickly become a premier spot for general work-related searching, including going through the online classifieds that many newspapers host. This is because of the myriad of work possibilities that one can now look through courtesy of digital technology. It's handy to go habitually through the many job listing spots on the Web, whether you're in desperate need of a job or "just browsing" for a change of pace.

Prior to the Net and the creation of such Web-based work listings as the well-known "Monster Board," one was, of course, essentially left with looking through their local papers or perhaps specialized trade journals to look for "help wanted" advertisements. Even with national trade journals, these type of "hard copy listings" were lacking in the kind of geographical and work-function comprehensiveness made possible by the Net. Now, postings arrive on a variety of Web sites daily, if not hourly, and they run the searchable range from geographical location to the kind of work you're looking for.

And this is just the beginning of the benefits of job-hunting via the Net.

Internet Explosion

With the rapid growth of the Net, the number of persons and organization who are posting "help wanted" notices on the Net has also markedly increased. In fact, the explosion of employment listings on the Net is most likely on its way to making the World Wide Web the largest job hunting market in the world. Also, many positions, both current and future, are listed exclusively on the Net. So if you don't look there, you really will be left in the dark.

Free Access to Premium Information

In may ways, there is no more valuable information in the world for an individual than information on a decent job. For the most part, we all must work for a living, but it helps if we can find a job that relatively suits us and pays good money. The Net can help you find the right job, and most employment hunting resources available on the Net are completely free to job hunters.

Free Dissemination of Your Information

For those "oldtimers" out there (read: over thirty), you may well remember copying hundreds of résumés, writing many individual cover letters, getting work samples in order, and mailing all of that in the hopes of hearing back a month later. Well, in almost one fell swoop, the Net allows you to post résumés and seamlessly send along work samples to a myriad of different employers (all of whom are hiring) at the literal push of a button (a mouse, to be specific).

An Open Job Market Twenty-Four Hours a Day

Often, job hunting opportunities can be limited by the fact that one is stuck from 9 A.M. to 5 P.M. in another job that one is anxious to take leave of. With the various job listings on the Net, one can comprehensively look to their heart's content and send along materials to potential employers—at any time of the day or night.

The World is Your Oyster

As we mentioned earlier, the scope of potential employment accessible via the Net is literally global. And while one may want something in their hometown, there will not only be listings from close to home, but also from elsewhere. So if you're inclined to relocate, then the Net can open that door for you. Also, the Net helps with long distance communications with your prospective employer by virtue of the fact that you can communicate by e-mail.

Employment Surf's Up

The following listing of employment Web sites takes a look at some of the top spots, but is by no means comprehensive of the job hunting resources that exist on the Net.

CareerPath.com http://careerpath.com

One of the original of the comprehensive job hunting Web sites, the CareerPath.com site is still one of the best. It posts an estimated 350,000 new jobs on its Net locale each and every month, and it is updated daily with feeds from newspapers across the United States. Jobs listed here are searchable by job category, by keyword, or by the newspaper that initially listed the job.

Also, CareerPath.com recently began featuring employer profiles where one can research on "mini-homepages" that have information on companies that one might be interested in.

Monster Board www.monsterboard.com/

This site is international in scope, but naturally, one can narrow searches down to something more specific than just "the world." And there are separate, smaller boards, such as "Monster Board UK," which allow definitive searches in that particular country.

American in origin, however, the Monster Board is most comprehensive when it comes to jobs in the good old U.S. of A., where one can go from town to town looking at what's available or just type in a job title and see what happens. In addition to listing employment, the Board allows job hunters to post résumés to a central bulletin board. This essentially reverses the job hunting process (which isn't a bad thing) in that when you post your résumé, employers can find *you* when they're searching for staff. But as most veteran job hunters, on and off the Net, will advise, take action; don't just wait for potential employers to find you.

CareerMosaic www.careermosaic.com/

This Web site is another instance of Net pages doing some of the hard work of job hunting for you, by virtue of the fact that CareerMosaic is focused on building a searchable database of résumés. Potential employers pay CareerMosaic for access to the myriad of résumés that are hosted here in order to find potential staff that fits their needs.

And you get to post your résumé for free. But don't just send in your résumé and forget about it, as Mosaic will keep your résumé for only three months.

America's Job Bank www.ajb.dni.us/

This Netlocale is hosted courtesy of the U.S. Labor Department and is paid for by Uncle Sam. It, naturally, lists jobs only available in the United States. But within that particular scope, there is quite a bit one can find. A recent check of America's Job Bank showed that there were 250,000 jobs listed, which means that the Job Bank has even more employment opportunities available than the more international Monster Board. And many observers have said that Job Bank has one of the more efficient job search engines of any employment Web site.

The Job Bank does lack, however, some of the extra features that one finds at some of the private services, such as allowing résumé postings and the kind of question-and-answer facility from job hunting "experts" that some Web sites boast.

College Grad Job Hunter www.collegegrad.com

This site is, as its name implies, devoted to helping those who face upcoming graduation and getting work. Quite simple in its operation, one just enters a job category ("writer," for instance) and the Job Hunter search engine will then list the names of companies that have employment opportunities in that category.

Also included in this site are helpful "how to" tips on résumé and cover letter writing, along with advice on how to get your résumé passed around and otherwise noticed. And there are suggestions on how to dress for your interviews as well.

CHAPTER 14

Looking for Legal Information

N et lawyers and law resources are coming of age. The volume of legal information available via the Internet several years ago was at best marginal, but this situation has been aptly remedied over the last two years, with everything from the U.S. Code to various lists of lawyers now accessible on the Net. One can also find circuit court decisions, many police records, university law departments and their law libraries; and many law firms have some kind of presence on the Web. U.S. Supreme Court decisions can be researched at a number of Web sites, including one that has archives of court decisions extending back to 1936.

Lawyer Josh Blackman, author of *How to Use the Internet for Legal Research* and editor of the *Internet Lawyer* newsletter (*www. internetlawyer. com*), views the Net as a growing alternative to the common legal practice of using expensive databases such as Lexis-Nexis. "The Internet, in particular, offers many new and valuable ways to conduct research," Blackman said. "For example, one can access documents from central collections created by lawyers and law librarians, one can access databases provided for free by public and private organizations, and one can use the Net to find experts for consultative purposes."

Among the top legal resource Web sites that Blackman recommends is the FindLaw site (*www.findlaw.com*), which has not only a comprehensive series of hyperlinks to information on state, federal, and international law, but also a legal-specific search engine called LawCrawler.

A top spot for jumping into the legal fray is the American Bar Association (ABA) Web site (*www.abanet.org*), which has not only an extensive compilation of legal links, but also much content on the site itself, in the form of articles for various ABA publications and position papers on ABA policy.

Another top starting spot for any kind of legal research is the Cornell Law School Legal Information Institute (*www.law.cornell.edu/*), which made earlier use of the Net to publish legal material in order to foster research via this medium. It continues to provide an excellent, broadranging resource that is most often cited for the access that it provides to Supreme Court documents. To search specifically through the syllabi of Supreme Court decisions, go to *www.law.cornell.edu/supct/*.

Also highly recommended is the U.S. House of Representatives Internet Law Library (*http://law.house.gov/*), which started life as a proprietary online service solely for the use of House staff, but is now publicly available to all, courtesy of the Net. Among other resources found here is the entirety of the U.S. Code and the Code of Federal Regulations.

Judicial Branch

If you wish to travel through the judicial branch of the United States Government, starting with the Supreme Court and then the circuit courts, the list below will provide you with a guidepost. I've omitted links to the state court system, as that would be too voluminous. However, a link to the National Center for State Courts is provided.

- U.S. Court of Appeals, Federal Circuit *www.law.emory.edu/ fedcircuit*
- District of Columbia Circuit *www.ll.georgetown.edu/Fed-Ct/ cadc.html*

- 1st Circuit *www.law.emory.edu/1circuit/*
- 2nd Circuit *www.law.pace.edu/legal/us-legal/judiciary/second-circuit.html*
- 3rd Circuit *www.law.vill.edu/Fed-Ct/ca03.html*
- 4th Circuit *www.law.emory.edu/4circuit*
- 5th Circuit *www.ca5.uscourts.gov/*
- 6th Circuit *www.law.emory.edu/6circuit*
- 7th Circuit *www.law.emory.edu/7circuit*
- 8th Circuit *www.wulaw.wustl.edu/8th.cir/*
- 9th Circuit *www.law.vill.edu/Fed-Ct/ca09.html*
- 10th Circuit *www.law.emory.edu/10circuit/*
- 11th Circuit *www.mindspring.com/~wmundy/opinions.html*

State Courts
- National Center for State Courts *www.ncsc.dni.us*

Law School Web Sites
- Brooklyn Law School (New York) *http://brkl.brooklaw.edu/*
- Chicago Kent-ITT School of Law *www.kentlaw.edu/*
- Columbia University Law Library (New York) *http://pegasus.law.columbia.edu/*
- Dickinson School of Law (Pennsylvania) *http://206.102.94.190/*
- Fordham University Law Library (New York) *http://lawpac.fordham.edu*
- George Washington University Law Library (Washington, D.C.) *http://128.164.161.3/*
- Georgetown University Law Library (District of Columbia) *http://141.161.38.45/*
- Howard University Law Library (Washington, D.C.) *http://library.law.howard.edu/*
- Indiana University School of Law *www.law.indiana.edu/law/lawindex.html*
- Loyola University Law School (California) *http://157.242.152.7/*
- McGeorge Law School (California) *http://138.9.150.10/*

- New York Law School *http://lawlib.nyls.edu*
- New York University Law School *http://julius.nyu.edu*
- South Texas College of Law of Texas A&M University *http://stexl.stcl.edu*
- Southern Illinois University School of Law *http://131.230.102.1/*
- Texas A&M University Law Center *http://stexl.stcl.edu/screens/opacmenu.html*
- University of California–Berkeley: Boalt Hall School of Law *www.law.berkeley.edu/institutes/*
- University of Colorado Law Library *http://lawpac.colorado.edu/*
- University of Connecticut Law School *http://137.99.202.99/*
- Yale University Law School (Connecticut) *http://130.132.84.29*

Other

- American Law Sources Online *www.lawsource.com/also/*
- Martindale-Hubbell Lawyer Locator *www.martindale.com*
- The Practicing Attorney's Home Page *www.legalethics.com/pa/main.html*
- West's Legal Directory *www.wld.com/*

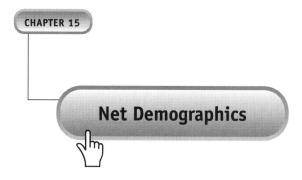

CHAPTER 15

Net Demographics

One thing is indeed certain about Internet demographics—nothing is for certain. The Net's impact is felt around the world as it breaks down traditional communication barriers and replaces them with a free-flowing information network.

Past, Present, and Future

Over the last decade, the Internet has grown exponentially, and it has propelled us into the emerging Information Age of the 1990s and beyond. Because of continual and rapid growth, qualifying and quantifying this emerging infrastructure has proven very difficult.

What makes the Net so chaotic is its immensity and intangibility. Its users and content are practically immeasurable—in both numbers and organization. Net users' identities are disguised by cryptic e-mail addresses, and online content is known more by word-of-mouth rather than a grand master index. Discovering a Web site you like is often more an exercise in serendipity than a planned excursion. This scenario, however, is natural to a phenomenon such as the Internet that has no central organizing body. After all, nobody actually owns the Internet, per se, but as commerce becomes more popular online, fractions of the network will establish property rights. Unlike the traditional kind of property rights we're used to that allow owners to build a home or a shop, such rights on the Internet will be virtual, composed of bits of data and computer memory.

Already becoming commonplace is Internet-based commerce that is almost as easy as calling a 1-800 number from a catalog. But will it take a generation before using the Internet is as much a part of our everyday lives as using the microwave? A recent study showed that the microwave is the most widely used technological innovation over the last twenty-five years. Sound surprising? Maybe not, if you consider what people really value out of technology (making their lives easier by automating everyday tasks). The true measure of any technology's effectiveness comes down to how much time it saves its users.

As for self-publicity, the Net is getting tremendous media attention. The number of stories about the Net in selected United States newspapers, news magazines, and television news broadcasts has increased from just 57 in February 1992 to nearly 12,000 stories in February 1998 (DowJones).

But if we sift through the hype, we realize that the Internet is still inaccessible—financially, geographically, and even psychologically—to large portions of the world population. In response to this dilemma, businesses are finding ways to get more people online and comfortable with the experience.

As an increasing amount of commercial enterprises inhabit the Net, they will instinctively find creative ways to make order out of the cyberchaos. Computer programmers will essentially become cartographers of the Internet, mapping our journeys and experiences through thousands of sites on the information superhighway, just as companies like Rand McNally and DeLorme do for our asphalt highways. Directory services, like those provided for phone numbers, will be essential for keeping track of online content. Soon everything from Net-user tracking to demographic studies to intelligent Net assistants will make the online universe start to look very different—and perhaps quite commonplace.

Grandiose visions of online commerce have been the impetus for

Internet demographic studies. Just as consumers of all other forms of media (print, radio, television) have been thoroughly categorized for marketing analyses, the growing online population will be qualified and quantified. As the Internet exploded over the last two years with the introduction of the World Wide Web's graphical user interface, companies from MCI to Nike to your local florist now recognize its vast potential and are anxious to tap your online dollars.

Like any other medium, demographic information to find out who's online is necessary for effective marketing strategies. Until recently, however, such studies didn't exist because Internet anonymity made it difficult to tell if users were male or female, black or white, young or old. Early efforts didn't even attempt to qualify these basic characteristics. They merely quantified the Internet's size by examining domains and hosts on the network. (A domain is the unique name identifying any site online, and a host is a computer on a network that provides Internet services, such as World Wide Web or Usenet, to other computers on the network.)

In one early study, researchers developed a special program to search the entire global Internet and retrieve data from all known domains and hosts. This analysis provided growth statistics from 1981 to 1991. They discovered 900 domains in 1981; 4,800 in 1986; and 17,000 in 1991. They also found 213 Internet hosts in 1981; 5,089 hosts in 1986; and by 1991, there were a staggering 727,000 hosts.

By the early 1990s, when this study was completed, demographers had found ways to identify online users by basic characteristics such as gender. What they found was a very skewed audience—the ratio of men to women was about 9:1. But by 1993, when the World Wide Web was introduced and attracted widespread interest, the gender gap showed signs of breaking down. Recent findings from large-scale surveys show an almost even split.

One of the most respected of the various Internet surveys is the ongoing poll conducted by Georgia Tech. Findings from their eighth in a regular series of surveys show the following:

Georgia Tech's GVU Center's Eighth World Wide Web Study Fact Sheet (1997)

- 38.4 percent of Internet users are female and 61.5 percent are male
- 66 percent of all Internet users in 1995 had a college degree compared to 47 percent in 1997
- 50 percent of all users had less than 12 months of experience on the Internet in 1995 compared with 37 percent in 1997
- There are more female users (11 percent) in the 16–20 age group than males (8 percent)
- 84 percent of all users say the Internet is indispensable
- 84 percent of long-time users have shopped on the Internet as opposed to 54 percent of new users
- 50 percent of all shoppers on the Internet leave sites because the system is too slow—68 percent of long-time users get impatient with speed while shopping as opposed to 38 percent of novices
- 31 percent of all Internet users were employed in the computer field in 1995 versus 21 percent in 1997
- 41 percent of Internet users access the system from home only
- In the 19–25 year-old age range, 49 percent use the Internet for activities related to education
- The number of people over fifty using the Internet increased from 11 percent in 1995 to 14 percent in 1997
- 41 percent of people over fifty say the Internet makes them feel more connected to family members
- Yahoo is the most popular Web site on the Internet
- Privacy has replaced censorship as the number-one policy concern of all Internet users
- Slow speed is the number-one technical concern of all Internet users

Note: The term "Internet users" in the above information refers to the 10,000 respondents who participated in the GVU World Wide Web Survey.

Survey results can be found at: *www.gvu.gatech.edu/user_surveys/.*

Other recent studies, like their earlier counterparts, focus on technical demographics. These studies show there are over one million computer systems now connected to the global Internet. The most popular online activity is electronic mail, with over 100 million e-mail messages exchanged every day, along with millions of files, graphics, sounds, and even video.

With such a phenomenal rate of growth, consumer demographics companies are getting into the game by conducting market research for corporations with Net sites. Nielsen, for example, has started to do for the Internet what it has done for television for years. The folks at Nielsen found Internet users to be well-educated, with 64 percent having a college degree, compared to 28 percent of the general population. Perhaps most importantly, the study found that 2.5 million people engage in online commerce activities. Such proof of buying products and services online is a valuable indication that an online marketplace currently exists and is viable. Finally, they compared surveys conducted online to those, like their own, done offline. This was used to examine the inherent bias among the online sample who volunteer to fill out the survey as opposed to a random sample of people who don't initiate participation. Such self-selection results in less accurate statistics.

The fact is that most Internet users prefer to stay anonymous while online, indeed a very important reason for the Net's popularity. Let's say, for example, that you're a shy person who is hesitant to voice your opinions to strangers. But when you're in the privacy of your own home, sitting in front of your computer, and you sign on to your favorite newsgroup, you avoid the traditional kind of societal intimidation you may encounter on the street. None of your online colleagues can see or hear you, so you feel free to speak your mind. This phenomenon transcends all social factors that influence how people behave among others, such as socioeconomic status, race, gender, or age. These everyday characteristics are completely meaningless in the online world. Nobody can judge you because of who or what you are—only simply by what you have to say. Such an ideal, pure situation is understandably very attractive to many people.

A variety of current estimates show the worldwide Internet population at over 200 million people, about the size of a large European country. With enough people now online to create their own society, the rush to claim one's own parcel of land in cyberspace is increasingly important, especially for commercial entities. Title to cyberland involves registering "domain names," the labels that identify Internet sites. Companies use the *.com* domain, which classifies them as commercial.

If current growth trends continue, the information superhighway will double in size about every one or two years. Experts agree that the majority of people in developed countries will be using the Net regularly by the year 2000. But just exactly who, what, why, where, when, and how these people are using the Internet will be answered by the new cyber-demographers. Recent surveys show online activities vary greatly (from playing games to job hunting, using electronic mail, reading novels, or just having fun "surfing" the Net). The challenge for the future will be to qualify who's doing each of these activities and why.

With a solid demographic understanding of the online population, the Internet can reach its full potential. More and more companies will become comfortable with the technology and learn how to take advantage of this new medium. Electronic commerce will flourish and bring with it the money and resources needed to make the Internet a truly global and accessible network. As it reaches maturity, the Net will become fully cataloged and mapped, perhaps even replacing the microwave as the most efficient and useful new technology.

For an excellent index of Internet demographics URLs, point your browser to this address: *www.yahoo.com/Computers_and_Internet/ Internet/Statistics_and_Demographics/*.

SECTION III

Journalism Research

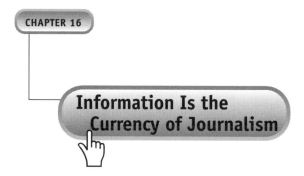

CHAPTER 16

Information Is the Currency of Journalism

"The information explosion is creating shell-shocked newsrooms," said longtime news librarian Nora Paul, during a presentation at a recent NetMedia conference in London. Paul is the director of the Poynter Institute library and heads the news research and news library management seminars. Prior to joining Poynter in 1991 she was with the *Miami Herald* for twelve years.

With over two decades of newsroom observation to draw upon, Paul notes that electronic fact gathering has changed things considerably for both news librarians and for news reporters. "Newsrooms, which fifteen years ago dealt with a single medium (paper), limited resources (clips from their own publications and some books), and simple technology (microfilm readers), are now being strafed with possibilities, choices, and ever-changing technologies," Paul said.

For news librarians, gone are the days of clipping articles from their newspapers for the morgue, and doing reference work. For reporters, there is a new and increased responsibility to become information researchers in their own right.

In emphasizing the importance of research to news operation, Paul likes to quote novelist John Katzenbach, who said "information is the currency of journalism." She adds that getting information is often the largest budget item of a newsroom's expense ledger and that it's getting even bigger.

"Whether it is information gathered from interviewing and reporting, Web pages located through searching the Internet, documents found in a commercial database search, public records examined through use of spreadsheets, or chapters in a book," Paul said, "the cost of acquiring, searching, and maintaining information in newsrooms is growing each year." But the cost for missing key information can be even higher in terms of losing out to other newsgatherers, according to Paul.

"The competitive edge will go to the newsroom with the quickest and ablest access to the facts, background, and sources that can give them the freshest angle, the deepest understanding and the broadest interpretation of news events," she warns. To keep up, Paul said, newsrooms must do more than just invest in the latest hardware and software; they need to allocate money "to upgrade the wetware (people)." In many newsrooms there is a commitment to the necessary training in order to keep the staff information-savvy. But Paul said that more must be done in terms of training for technical and research skills.

To see what resources the Poynter Institute has available, go to *www.poynter.org*. Nora Paul can be reached at *npaul@poynter.org*.

The meeting of computers and reporters requires new news strategies. Newsrooms need a new structure and coverage strategy for the new age of information, Brant Houston told fellow journalists at the recent NetMedia conference in London. Houston is the managing director of the National Institute for Computer-Assisted Reporting, which is based in the Journalism School at the University of Missouri.

The traditional management structure of publisher, editor, and reporter, and the fiefdoms of the national, state, and city desk, are failing to work together in today's dynamic information environment that has been forged by electronic databases and the Internet. Also (and equally important) the departmental separation between newsroom and library must be bridged, said Houston.

"In addition to sometimes inhibiting communication and cooperation, the structure also makes few arrangements for training for reporters and editors," Houston said. "The editors, in particular, are put at a disadvantage because they must increasingly make critical decisions concerning new information gathering techniques and choose hardware, software . . . without a good working knowledge of the techniques and technology."

Houston harked back to the traditional method of work in newsrooms, where, upon returning from his "beat," a reporter would archive notes and other information in his or her private files. "If a reporter shares this information, it is generally on an informal basis in conversation," Houston said. "Indeed, some reporters see little sense in sharing too much information because of the internal competitiveness in a newsroom."

Secondary sources, such atlases, directories, reports, and archived news stories, usually are stored in the news library, whose librarian "then works hard to remind the news staff of the documents and resources that have been gathered," Houston said.

The advent of various electronic sources, such as databases that hold census information, public employee salary data, medical statistics, and housing profiles, has made the news library (and those able to work with this material) an increasingly important resource. According to Houston, a new structure for newsrooms would, in part, include closer work between research librarians, reporters, and editors, and would require more research and technology training for newsroom staff.

"Once formed, these new teams of specialists would then work together to coordinate the acquisition of information, its storage, its distribution and its use for news stories," Houston said. He cites the example of a reporter who, in the new information environment, might put his or her interview material into a software program such as Lotus Notes, where it can be retrieved easily later by doing keyword searches. In turn, this information can be easily shared. Also, a news librarian who tracks each reporter's beat can keep them posted electronically when relevant new material arrives into the news organization's databases.

To peruse further information about NICAR go to *www.nicar.org.*

CHAPTER 17

Covering National Issues

"In order to be competitive, journalists need information more quickly than ever before," says Judith Doherty, National and International Editor of the *Washington Post*'s online edition.

Indeed, the journalist writing national stories is often faced with the challenge of researching huge events or topics under the same deadline constraints as local reporters. Education, welfare, transportation—these subjects create piles of paperwork, support an array of experts and critics, and sometimes take weeks to grasp. So what's an industrious journalist to do?

Employ the Internet as a research tool. Multiple national story ideas, case studies, government documents, and other important sources can be found on the Net. The growing appeal of Internet-assisted reporting attests to the advantages journalists have enjoyed by using it. The 1997 Media in Cyberspace Study reports that 93 percent of journalists are using the Internet at least occasionally, and the number of publications now offering online versions has doubled in two years.

The report (available at *http://mediasource.com*) is one of the largest surveys conducted concerning online journalism, with more than 2,500 respondents. According to the report, "almost all journalists now use online tools for researching and reporting."

With that in mind, the best way to find out how journalists use the Internet to cover national issues is to ask them. By examining how today's journalists use the Internet, and which sites they find most helpful, any researcher can be more successful online.

Before Starting Your Research

Although it's tempting, most experienced Internet researchers don't suggest jumping directly online without a plan.

"The Internet is sprawling, and unless you can narrow your search, you're not going to find what you need," says Steven Ross, Associate Professor at Columbia University's Graduate School of Journalism and co-author of the Media in Cyberspace Study. Ross notes that many self-proclaimed Internet experts don't know how to efficiently use this tool. His suggestions: establish a clear research plan and hypothesis before logging on, and learn how to use Boolean operators to refine your research. "Learning how to use the tool is critical to getting the most out of it," Ross cautions.

Cathy Hayden, Education Reporter at the *Clarion-Ledger* in Jackson, Mississippi, discovered how successful educated Web searches can be when she started a project on national teacher shortages. "I learned that part of it is how you define an issue," Hayden says. By searching for teacher shortage information in a variety of ways—teacher supply, teacher quality, teacher recruitment—she found more useful information than if she had just used "teacher shortage" as her key word search. Using multiple search engines is another common practice of smart Internet researchers. Each engine is created differently. Using the same key word search on several engines will result in a variety of selected sites, so it's always a better idea to try a few different engines if you're not finding what you're looking for.

Besides learning how to use the Internet, organizing what you need to know is also critical to doing online research, says Alan Schlein, journalist and owner of the Deadline Online consulting firm. Schlein suggests structuring research questions according to the standard, but sometimes overlooked, journalistic format of who, what, when, where, why, and how. "We take for granted that we know how to look for information once we're online," Schlein says. "But unfortunately, it's easy for the well-meaning reporter to get lost on the Internet without a research plan." Taking a few minutes to define the questions you're trying to answer may help you stay focused.

Surveying Current National News Stories

Many journalists admit that, when in need of a great story idea, the Internet is the perfect place to brainstorm. "National issues are easy to research online because there is so much material to begin with," says media consultant Tom Hendrick. Stumbling upon a story about a troubled city prison system may lead to comparative studies from other state and federal prisons nationwide. Glancing at the studies, a journalist may notice a pattern in prison rates or prison relocations, and within a few minutes a fresh story idea is born. "Each morsel leads me to a couple different things, and it multiplies," Hendrick says.

"Few reporters would work on a story of any sort now without checking the Net the way they routinely check the clips of their own newspaper or TV station," says Rosemary Armao, former Director of Investigative Reporters and Editors. Now at the *Baltimore Sun,* Armao believes that Internet research has moved into journalism completely, and computer-assisted reporting will become mainstream. But even if a journalist has no clear direction, "Web sources can be good sources of inspiration," says George Rodrigue. This reporter from the *Dallas Morning News* visits sites maintained by Washington-based think tanks to gather newsworthy reports and peruse archived speeches.

Steve Outing, president of the interactive media research and consulting firm Planetary News, guesses that more than half of his story ideas come from e-mails. "My column (at Editor and Publisher's Web site) includes my e-mail address, so I'm easy to reach." He recounts a story idea he gleaned from an anonymous e-mail: "Just recently, I got some great inside information about a company that was going through some troubles and just laid off about one-third of its staff. The sender worked there, but sent e-mail through an anonymous re-mailer to disguise his or her identity. I learned some important things from this person's e-mail that really helped my questioning when I conducted interviews with the company's executives."

Favorite sites for story ideas include: Excite's NewsTracker (*http://nt.excite.com*), which has links to current news articles and online publications; NewsBot (*www.wired.com/newsbot*), which searches for current news items; and News Index (*http://newsindex.com*), which lists breaking news stories and searches indexes from over 250 newspapers and news sources.

The Documents Center is a central reference for government information. Their political science resources page (*http://henry.ugl.lib.umich.edu/libhome/Documents.center/psnews.html*) has links to U.S. and foreign news sources, newspapers, newswires, and a lot more. The American Journalism review (*www.newslink.org*) has links to all U.S. papers and magazines that have Web sites. Hot News/Hot Research (*www.poynter.org/research/reshotres.htm*) is a Poynter Institute site that compiles breaking news story sites.

Editor and Publisher maintains an online list of newspapers and magazines at *http://mediainfo.elpress.com/ephome/npaper/nphtm/online.htm*. Public Agenda Online: The Journalist's Inside Source for Public Opinion and Policy Analysis (*www.publicagenda.org*) is a site summarizing national issues from education to abortion, and includes links to other public policy Web sites.

Finding Sources

"One of the great charms of the Internet is its ability to find sources," says Joseph Campbell, Associate Professor at American University's School of Communication. The Internet almost instantaneously links journalists to sources in any field, and most have e-mail accounts that are easily accessible. But Campbell warns that sources may not be as likely to respond to an e-mail as they would to a phone call. "For whatever reason, e-mails just aren't as real," Campbell says. "And what's the sanction if you don't respond?"

Nonetheless, e-mail is a blessing to journalists working under a dead-

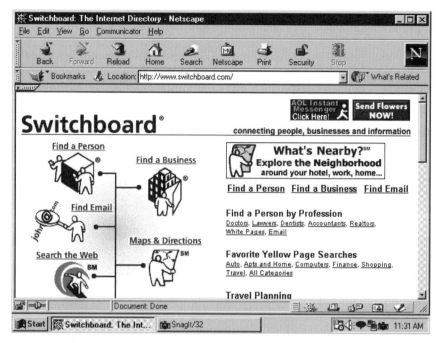

Where are they now? The peoplefinder engines can help find out.

line. George Rodrigue from the *Dallas Morning News* points out that e-mail is "a great way to keep in touch with sources, solicit expert opinions, tap into mailing lists of concern, and get press releases quickly." And many federal agencies and nonprofit organizations now distribute information via e-mail instead of fax or regular mail, making it much easier to get information about national issues fast.

Planetary News President Steve Outing believes that press releases are the "most handy" resources available on the Web. By doing a search on a site like PR Newswire, Outing can access press releases that include names, phone numbers, and e-mail addresses of public relations officials. "In those instances where my Rolodex fails me, this is a real time saver—and it sure beats calling up the company's main phone number and having to go through some clueless receptionist," he says. Outing also uses mailing lists to survey large numbers of people. By posting a general question or request, interested people can respond to him through a private e-mail. "I often turn up sources this way that I wouldn't have known about otherwise," Outing says.

A warning: Don't become so dependent on your online sources that you forget to talk to real human beings. Columbia's Steve Ross worries that new information technology has become so easy to use that journalists may settle into a pattern of lazy reporting. Joseph Campbell agrees that, all too often, reporters give up on a story idea, saying, "Well, I didn't find anything on the Web. . . ." While the Internet can be a great place to start looking for contacts, phone and in-person conversations are still a wonderful way to collect information and maintain the human element in a story.

Favorite sites for finding sources include PR Newswire's media-only Web site (*www.prnmedia.com*), which searches for company press releases available online, and the MegaSources page (*www.megasource. com*), which provides links to source-finder sites, expert yearbooks, and search indexes.

Phonebook Gateway (*www.uiuc.edu/cgi-bin/ph*) searches over three hundred phonebook servers, while Anywho Directory Service (*www. anywho.com*) searches telephone books, reverse directories, and maps. Four11 (*www.four11.com*) can search for e-mail addresses and has white and yellow phone book accessibility, as well as reverse directories. Switchboard (*www.switchboard.com*) will also search for people, businesses, and e-mail addresses.

The Online-news list is a public mailing list that allows journalists, researchers and other media-friendly folks to talk about the transition of news media into "new" media. To subscribe, send a message to *lyris@ planetarynews.com* and in the body of the message type "subscribe online-news" or visit the Web page at *www.planetarynews.com/online-news.*

ProfNet (*www.prnews.com*) can find experts from the thousands of university press offices nationwide. Include your affiliation, a specific description of the type of expert you're looking for, and questions you need answered. Expect an answer within forty-eight hours.

Reporter's Desktop (*www.seanet.com/~duff/*), created by the *Seattle Times'* Duff Wilson, includes links to government and press sites, as well as tools for searching for people, e-mail addresses, phone numbers, and other sources.

Fact-Checking and Reference Sites

All-encompassing reference sites on the Internet are quickly (and thankfully) replacing dictionaries, encyclopedias, indexes, and other ominous tomes of information. "I've looked up everything from the budget to the Bible to Shakespeare to Rabelais in recent weeks," says Jodie Allen, Washington editor of Slate magazine. "Same stuff we used to get from the library... only faster," she says, and that's the beauty of the Internet. By maneuvering quickly through information online, fact-checking that used to take several days in the library can take several hours.

Quick Internet searches have saved more than one reporter facing the ever-present deadline. Ray Gibson from the *Chicago Tribune* says that most investigative reporters turn to the Internet for last-minute help. "I was doing a story on our gubernatorial campaign finances and suddenly realized I didn't have one of the candidates' first reports that I needed to provide accurate numbers in my story," Gibson recounts. "Fortunately, [the candidate] had posted them on his Web site," saving Gibson from an embarrassing omission in his story. Even when you think the information you need couldn't possibly be online, check anyway. New reference sites are popping up everyday, many with very specific, and sometimes obscure, information.

Favorite reference sites include: FastFacts 1998 (*www.refdesk.com/ fastfact.html*), a virtual reference desk with hundreds of useful links, including maps, almanacs, dictionaries, encyclopedias, and many U.S. newspapers; the Virtual Reference Desk (*www.refdesk.com/main.html*), another multipurpose page with links to news, radio, papers, and more; the Scout Report (*http://scout.cs.wisc.edu/scout*), a compilation of Internet-based resources chosen by librarians and educators; and the University of Waterloo's Electronic Library site (*www.lib.uwaterloo.ca/ society/overview.html*), which has links to more than 1,100 scholarly societies and resource centers on the Internet.

Other reference sites of note include: States.org (*www.states.org*), a clearinghouse for tracking state information infrastructure activities; FACSNET (*www.facsnet.org*), which provides Internet resources, reporting tools, and online source information; and Deadline Online (*www.deadlineonline.com*), a customized program journalists use to find various information online.

Amazon.com (*www.amazon.com*) is not only an online bookstore, but an easy way to search for books by title, author, or keyword. It also has reviews.

Getting Access to Government Records

Many national reporters not familiar with political beats lament having to cover a government story. More than just the bureaucratic red tape, journalists find that many federal and state government agencies don't manage their information well, on- or offline. Cathy Hayden, from Mississippi's *Clarion-Ledger*, points out that some government Web sites aren't well maintained. "Our state Department of Education has a Web site listing employees, recent press releases, and upcoming events," she says, "but updating is spotty."

In general, though, local, state, and federal governments have come a long way toward making information readily accessible. The *Dallas News*'s George Rodrigue notes that Congress is getting more Internet-savvy. "Most of us have been using THOMAS, the legislative resource site, for some time," he says. "Now committees are putting hearing notices and witness statements up," making it easier to get information about particular legislative activities. Keep in mind that many government-related documents are public information. If the data you're looking for is not online, you may need to file a Freedom of Information Act request to obtain what you need. Many journalism sites have procedures for filing a request, including the Society of Professional Journalists, which maintains the Electronic Journalist FOI Resource Center (*http://spj.org/foia*), with information about government records. Also, Fed World Information Network has links to government agencies, reports and databases at its site: *www.fedworld.gov*.

Find Out What Journalists Are Doing Online

Ultimately, the best way to stay on top of the latest Internet research techniques is to maintain an online presence. Whether that means joining a mailing list or frequenting some of the sites specifically created for online journalists, knowing what your colleagues are doing can help you complete more thorough research. The Internet is always changing. Keeping that in mind should compel any competitive journalist to continuously watch the technology, and adapt to it as it improves.

The *Online Journalism Review* (*www.onlinejournalism.org*) reports on the latest issues affecting this new medium. The site is produced by the Annenberg School of Communication at the University of Southern California. Along with general resources, links to information about computer-assisted reporting and research can be found at the Computer-Assisted Reporting page (*www.ryerson.ca/~dtudor/carcarr.htm*). The Online Press Club/Journalism Forum provides online media professionals a chance to network at *www.jforum.org*. Also, the National Institute for Computer Assisted Reporting (*www.nicar.org*) maintains a site with links to CAR resources.

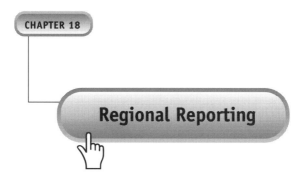

CHAPTER 18

Regional Reporting

T he Internet hasn't just improved the reporting and researching process for journalists working on large, national beats. Ernie Slone,
technology editor for the *Orange County Register*, has found that the
Internet also makes local stories much easier and quicker to cover.

"First, and probably foremost, is that online access to agencies and
organizations has given journalists much wider and easier access to
data," says Slone. Just several years ago, state and federal agencies
stored information on mainframe tapes. "If you wanted to get a list of
restaurants and their health ratings, you had to buy a nine-track tape,
have a $6,000 machine that could read it, and then have that tape drive
hooked up to a $3,000 computer," Slone says.

Information, even large quantities of it, can now be downloaded
online, saving the newsroom from having to purchase more expensive
mainframe equipment. By using file transfer protocol (FTP), data about
education, health, and thousands of other disciplines are more accessible. Slone explains: "Instead of arriving in some mainframe foreign
language like EBCDIC, the data is often ready to use in the form of a
spreadsheet or database."

Easy access to information allows the *Register*, based in Santa Ana,
California, to run several stories a week based on such data. "We get

school test scores, EPA air quality ratings, city budgets, contract information, cell-phone usage . . . the entire gamut of 'official' information this way in a continual stream," Slone says.

Slone suggests journalists build bookmarks to sites essential to their beats. "The reporter who makes it a regular practice to track the best sites is far more likely to be able to use the Net on deadline than someone who relies on last-minute searches."

What most reporters don't know, Slone confides, is that the best information you can get via the Net is not posted on the Net. "When you do a search of the Internet, you can find only information live on a Web page. But most of the best databases are not posted on the Web." Instead, savvy researchers know to go to a particular Web site, such as the National Institutes of Health, and fill in a form to look for relevant reports or studies. The query searches the NIH database for information that's not available live on the Net. "When the query finds a match in the offline database," Slone says, "the site builds a Web page on the fly with the information."

Slone gives an example: "I could go to the NIH site and find out how likely a person is to die in a car wreck versus dying of cancer or heart disease. But I can't get those numbers from a general Internet query at AltaVista or Yahoo. The data is out there, but you have to be able to locate the right path to it, via a Web site. So bookmarks are essential."

Although the Internet is dangerously convenient, Slone warns against depending on online information alone. "You should never settle for what is posted online," Slone says. "Frequently, much more information is available, but the agency or organization only puts up summary numbers or national figures."

Again, Slone gives an example from his own reporting experience: "Every time I see a national study with data, I automatically assume there are numbers for my county, city, and possibly even neighborhood or ZIP code. When the EPA released a report showing metro areas and how many days a year they violate air quality standards, I knew that the national report had to be generated from more local data. A critical step in using the Net most effectively is to contact a real person behind the site and find out if more specific data is available."

When Slone contacted the site, he found that the EPA not only had city numbers, but also had hourly numbers from each monitoring station in the county. "This is the single best tip I can give to any reporter about using the Net to cover local or regional issues," Slone says. "Talk to the people behind the site. Never settle for what's posted online."

Slone says the Internet also allows people to respond to stories online, "giving you fresh angles to pursue." He recalls the stories the *Register* ran about a 1995 fertility clinic scandal at the University of California at Irvine. A Mexican health official found the story online, after doing an Internet search on a doctor he intended to license. The official called Slone when he discovered that the doctor he was considering was the same doctor who fled to Mexico after allegedly stealing embryos from the UCI clinic. "Because we had a Web site," Slone says, "we made a valuable contact that led to additional stories." Because of this and other scoops by the reporters at the *Register*, Slone and the rest of the journalists who worked on the fertility clinic story won a 1996 Pulitzer Prize for investigative reporting.

"But the Web is important not only to reach those outside the newsroom, but to coordinate the work of those inside as well," Slone says. Last fall, Slone built an Intranet, accessible only to the *Register*'s journalists, posting a wealth of information to be used for stories on El Niño. "When the torrential rain fell, and hills started sliding, our reporters could easily find trouble spots, locate those who previously had suffered similar fates, and find other important information quickly," Slone says. "They could also easily reach their colleagues, since beeper numbers and other contact info was only a click away."

The *Orange County Register* is a Freedom Communications, Inc. newspaper, with a circulation of approximately 356,520 copies daily. The paper's site is at *www.ocregister.com. Orange County Register* reporting on the UCI fertility scandal includes a number of articles on the topic, such as the one at this Net address: *www.ocregister.com/archives/ 1998/06/03/crimecourts/uci003w.shtml.*

CHAPTER 19

Newspaper Morgues (Archives)

Until recently it was unheard of for newspapers to publish on the Internet, let alone have archived morgues of past editions. As veteran journalists and news librarians know, the original morgues were a vast, hard copy filing system of cross-referenced articles that sat year-after-year, yellowing away in file cabinets.

Jumping forward to the present, there are thousands of newspapers throughout the world that are on the Net, and while many still have yet to make their archives available on the Web, there are a number of newspapers that allow for archival research of one kind or another. The list could be larger, but it is quickly growing.

Some papers, such as the *Washington Post* (*www.washingtonpost.com*) are searchable at no cost, and you can rummage through a decade of their archives. Most other papers only go back for several years, but for a fee. Those who want to research newspaper morgues on the Net (versus Lexis-Nexis) should note that there are a variety of fee structures available, with lower cost searches that usually come with subscriptions to that paper. This is handy to know, of course, if you are a subscriber or considering a subscription.

The Knight-Ridder group hosts what is considered by many to be the top spot for searching through news archives at *http://newslibrary.*

infi.Net. There are twenty-two newspapers available for searches, most of them for a fee. In general, the cost is $1.50 per article during business hours (6 A.M. to 6 P.M. during the work week) and 25¢ all other times. So it obviously pays to research through Knight-Ridder's archives during the off hours.

Also at a cost is the *Boston Globe* (*www.boston.com/globe/archives*), which allows searches through the last fifteen years of material written by the paper's staff writers. During business hours the price is $2.50 per article, and $1.50 all other times. Free, however, are brief citations of articles relevant to your search topic.

The *Los Angeles Times* (*http://latimes.com*) charges $1.50 per article at all times, but also allows for a flat $4.95-a-month rate that allows for up to ten stories. After that, the buck-fifty kicks in. Searches here go back to 1990.

The following seven newspapers allow free access to at least the last year of their material, if not back further, according to recent article written by *Washington Post* news librarian Margot Williams:

- *Sacramento Bee* (archived from July 15, 1996): *www.sacbee.com*
- *San Francisco Chronicle* (from Jan. 1, 1995): *www.sfgate.com*
- *Kansas City Star* (from Jan. 1, 1991): *www.kcstar.com*
- *St. Louis Post-Dispatch* (from Jan. 1, 1988): *www.stlnet.com*
- *Deseret (Utah) News* (from Jan. 1, 1996): *www.desnews.com*
- *Las Vegas Sun* (from Jan. 1, 1996): *www.lasvegassun.com*
- *Detroit News* (from July 1, 1995): *http://detnews.com*

Williams, along with student researchers from George Washington University, has prepared a lengthy, general list of newspapers with Internet-accessible archives (both pay and free) at *http://sunsite.unc.edu/slanews/internet/archives.html.*

SECTION IV

Academic Research

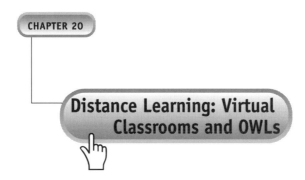

CHAPTER 20

Distance Learning: Virtual Classrooms and OWLs

All across the academic landscape, many students are attending classes, getting assignments and critiques, working with professors and fellow students, and ultimately getting degrees—all online. And while it is doubtful that entire campuses will close in favor of the cyberclassroom, there is a large trend afoot by most universities to offer entire virtual degree programs. A number of states are examining the creation of entire "virtual universities," which have no campus at all. These will be no fly-by-night academies and degree programs. The plans are for fully accredited institutions.

The Net has ushered in a new era in education that can prove of great benefit to all manner of scholars, including the far-flung tribe of writers and potential writers who want (or need) instruction but may be far afield from the institution or class of their choice.

"We're starting to see a revolution," said Nick Allen, the dean of Maryland's University College, to *Washington Post* reporter Rene Sanchez in a 1997 news article. "These are real classes and real degrees only a modem away."

What the Net replaces is the clunkier practice (though it had its place in history) of the "correspondence classes," where professors and students mail assignments and critiques, examinations and evaluations, back and forth via the U.S. Postal Service. Now with the expected ubiquity and efficiency of electronic and digital communications, the former small niche that distance learning occupied is starting to markedly expand.

The form that these online classes take are many. In some "virtual classes" the professor posts lecture notes and assignments on a central, electronic bulletin board accessible to the virtual students. Students can then use e-mail to make any queries to their professor and deliver finished assignments for grading. Other types of this new distance learning make even more progressive use of the Net by using "chat room" technology in order to actually have full online class meetings in real time. This also allows for group work on assignments.

There are also the "virtual reality" experiments which use MOO (Multi-user Object Oriented) and MUD (Multi-user Dimension) technology to allow for the illusion of students actually gathering within the same classroom, though it is actually in cyberspace. No doubt with the further perfection of virtual reality technology, the notion of distance learning may even come full circle to the point where, though the students and their respective professors are all geographically separated, everyone will seamlessly meet, discuss, and debate within the confines of the virtual class.

Whatever form that distance learning takes via the Net, there are already many opportunities to take online classes, in either entire online programs or a single accredited course.

For those who would like to read and study more on the growing practice of distance education, the University of Wisconsin-Extension program has created a Webguide and clearinghouse on the topic at *www.uwex.edu/disted/home.html*. Also helpful is the Distance Learning Resource Network at *www.fwl.org.edtech/dlrn.html*.

One of the earliest (and also quickly growing) manifestations of distance education are the myriad Online Writing Labs, or OWLs, that have been created or are being created by hundreds of schools. These are the natural technological extension of the kind of writers' workshops and individual tutorials that have existed for some time on campuses at many schools. One such writing lab, for instance, is the one that is hosted by Purdue University, at *http://owl.english.purdue.edu.* Dr. Muriel Harris, a founder of the Purdue OWL, had this to say, on her personal home page, about her school's Online Writing Lab and how it can benefit Purdue student writers and also writers-at-large:

"My interest in getting OWL to fly was that I want our Writing Lab to offer Purdue students (and others out there on the Internet) a desktop writing tool. OWL is a way to have easy access to our files of homemade instructional handouts, to contact us with questions or to talk about writing . . . I see OWL as a logical growth in our Writing Lab's services."

A quick review of the other OWLs on the Net show that Dr. Harris's comments stand true of the function and purpose of many OWLs. To some degree or another, each OWL offers the following:

- A conduit for communication between writing tutor and student
- A means of distributing learning resources (topical handouts) to student writers
- Allows for collaboration between students, and for group critiques of works
- A meeting place of like minds and talents
- Showcasing for student works and publications
- A jumping-off point for research into the greater Internet

Some other OWLs are:
- Bowling Green Online Writing Lab *www.bdsu.edu/departments/ writing-lab/*
- The Dakota State University OWL *www.dsu.edu/departments/lib- eral/owl*
- The University of Maine "Writing Center Online" *http://kramer. ume.maine.edu/~wcenter*
- The University of Michigan OWL *www.las.umich.edu/ecb/OWL/ owl.html*
- The University of Missouri's "Online Writery" *www.missouri.edu/ ~wleric/writery.html*
- Rensselaer Writing Center *www.rpi.edu/web/writingcenter/*

The National Writing Centers Association's OWL is located at *www2. colgate.edu/diw/NWCAOWLS.html*. Here, courtesy of Bruce Pegg at Colgate University (where the association is based), one can scroll through hundreds of hypertext links to various OWLs and writing centers. The list maintained here is searchable, alphabetically by school. Also hosted here is a large list of general resources available on the Internet for writers.

For Rebecca Rickly, OWL coordinator for the University of Michigan, the online tutoring made possible by the Net will allow not only for beneficial tutoring of U.M. students, but also for educational community outreach. "While the OWL is still evolving here, we're excited about the future. We see it as the center of a variety of other projects," she wrote about the creation of and changes to the OWL "For instance, we'd like to begin a cybermentoring program with an inner city Detroit high school. Where Michigan (U.M.) peer tutors establish an in-depth, one-on-one relationship with high school students, helping them not only with their writing, but introducing them to academic life from an insider's point of view."

Handouts

Besides providing an opportunity for registered student writers to attend classes long distance, many of these OWLs host freebies in the form of handouts, writing tips, and tutorials that are available to all interested parties at their respective Web sites.

As an example, the following is a short excerpt from a handout that was archived courtesy of the OWL at the University of Ohio:

On Stating a Theme in Literature

1. Theme must be expressible in the form of a statement with a subject and a predicate. It is insufficient to say that the theme of a story is motherhood or loyalty of country. These are simply the subjects. Theme must be a statement about the story's or poem's subject. If we express the theme in the form of a phrase, the phrase must be convertible to sentence form. A phrase such as "the futility of envy," for

instance, may be converted to the statement "Envy is futile": it may therefore serve as a statement of theme.

2. The theme must be stated as a generalization about life. In stating theme we do not use the names of the characters in the narrative, for to do so is to make a specific rather than a . . .

—Found at: *www.lima.ohio-state.edu/~WACC/WC-Handouts/lit-theme.txt*

This is just a brief example of the thousands of writing-tip handouts that have been made freely available by many of the OWLs. A further list of handouts at the Ohio State OWL includes how-to's on researching papers, guides to spelling, guides to rewriting and proofreading, a guide to résumé writing, and a guide to writing introductory paragraphs.

Educators who advocate the benefits of distance learning—and they seem to be a growing number—say that in addition to giving greater access to college courses in general, these courses are inherently less expensive because they are based in cyberspace. While not as ivy-covered as the traditional campus, these educational venues are also not beset with the problems of building maintenance.

CHAPTER 21

Literary Searching

" There are a million stories in the naked city—and this is just one of them."

The same could be said of the Internet and the number of writerly works and resources that are available.

The following is just one example of the many possible literary searches that can be conducted on the Net. In this case, we're looking for just one quote from the voluminous works of the bard William Shakespeare, Elizabethan playwright and poet.

During spring, as the ides of March approached, I began my hunt for Internet-based Shakespeariana on the Excite search engine (*www. excite.com*), using "ides of March and Shakespeare" under the concept search heading. I was looking for the author's *Julius Caesar*. But it took some hunting through various other Shakespeare-related resources until I actually found the desired "ides," which in turn enabled me to finally quote from the famous play for this chapter.

Looking for Shakespeare

Let us start with the site that ultimately led me to the passage I sought. It is called "Mr. William Shakespeare and the Internet" (*www.palomar.*

edu/Library/shake.htm) and proved to be one of the single best sites for studying and quoting the Bard. This is a relatively new site that has pledged itself to the purpose of listing the many informational links to Shakespeare text, criticism, and education. Also available from the Mr. William Shakespeare page are links to Elizabethan and Renaissance resources.

Terry Gray, the author of this excellent page, has annotated the links with personal commentary that is helpful as you navigate through the site looking for any particular morsel of information. He says this about his page in an opening message, "If you are a true Shakespearean, the term 'scholarly material' will translate as 'fun.' If you are being forced to take a Shakespeare class or do research, this is your chance to become a true Shakespearean and develop a love and enjoyment for the best poet ever."

Once there, some of the key links to other Web sites include Bartlett's Famous Shakespeare Quotations, a searchable index of Shakespearean sonnets and other poetry, and a searchable index of all Shakespeare. Also there is a link to answers for frequently asked questions (FAQ) about the man and a link to the Shakespeare Illustrated site, which boasts a variety of nineteenth-century oil paintings depicting scenes from the Bard's works.

Under the Renaissance category, there is a guide to proper Elizabethan pronunciations and access to a number of musical sites with sound files of Renaissance-era music. The available scholarly criticism of Shakespeare includes the writings of fellow Englishman Dr. Johnson and a link to the "Richard III society," where one can read a tract by scholar James A. Moore, Ph.D., entitled "Historicity in Shakespeare's *Richard III*." It is this particular passage that looks at the issues of Shakespeare's possible role as a Tudor propagandist:

> Throughout the 20th century, historians and literary critics have thoroughly understood the Tudor bias tainting the historicity of Shakespeare's sources for *Richard III*, not only as found in Thomas Moore's *History of Richard III*, but especially in the chronicles of Polydore Vergil, Edward Hall, and Raphael Holinshead . . .

Cursory examination of statements about Shakespeare in *The Ricardian* (17) reveals, by and large, a healthy respect for his genius. Seldom have they accused him with Thomas More and the Tudor chroniclers of being a deliberate propagandist for the Tudors. Furthermore, reviews of *Richard III* stage productions generally have focused upon dramatic merit rather than strictly upon historical deficiencies.

—Found at *www.Webcom.com/~blanchrd/bookcase/moore1.html*

Still on the quest for the "ides of March," I traveled from the Mr. William Shakespeare page to one of the most singularly interesting search engines on the Net—the Shakespeare Search page at the Massachusetts Institute of Technology.

As an aside, the reader should note that these "mini-search engines"—known as "wide area information searchers (or servers)," WAIS for short—actually pre-date the current crop of powerful engines such as AltaVista or Lycos, which search and index the entirety of the Web. It is at this MIT Internet address (*http://the-tech.mit.edu/cgi-bin/shakesearch.pl*), that I was able to quickly find references to the "ides" courtesy of the WAIS. Here, I not only found seven references to "ides," but also, by clicking on any one of them, was able to read the entirety of Shakespeare's *Julius Caesar*, in which these words are contained. Indeed, here at MIT are the entire texts of all of Shakespeare.

I clicked on the first reference and was taken to Act I, Scene 2 of *Julius Caesar*.

Flourish.

Enter CAESAR; ANTONY, for the course; CALPURNIA, PORTIA, DECIUS BRUTUS, CICERO, BRUTUS, CASSIUS, and CASCA; a great crowd following, among them a Soothsayer.

CAESAR: Set on; and leave no ceremony out.   *Flourish.*

SOOTHSAYER: Caesar!

CAESAR: Ha! who calls?

CASCA: Bid every noise be still; peace yet again.

CAESAR: Who is it in the press that calls on me?

    I hear a tongue, shriller than all the music.

Cry Caesar! Speak; Caesar is turned to hear.

SOOTHAYER: Beware the ides of March.

CAESAR: What man is that?

BRUTUS: A soothsayer bids you beware the ides of March.

—Found at *http://the-tech.mit.edu/Shakespeare/*

Tragedy/juliuscaesar/juliuscaesar.1.2.html

Of course, one can also just go directly to MIT's "Complete Works of William Shakespeare" home page, which allows one to click on a play by title, under the neatly categorized sections of Comedy, History, Tragedy, and Poetry. The Complete Works are at *http://the-tech.mit.edu/ Shakespeare/works.html.*

But not all my searches were so successful. When I began my search for the quote, the Excite search engine initially led me to the Shakespeare Oxford Society page (*www.shakespeare-oxford.com/*). This site, which boasts a solid compilation of Bard links, is actually devoted to the pursuit of questioning Shakespeare's authorship of the plays and sonnets that most experts think he wrote. Here's the opening message from the Society's home page: "The purpose of the Shakespeare Oxford Society is to document and establish Edward de Vere, 17th Earl of Oxford (1550–1604), as the universally recognized author of the works of William Shakespeare."

The mainstay of the Society's publishing efforts are its quarterly *Shakespeare Oxford Newsletter* (which is curious, considering they don't think Shakespeare is actually Shakespeare), a hard copy missive, and the *Ever Reader.* The latter is an online magazine that carries articles, news, debates, and bibliographies, which it claims "impart a wide range of corroborating information and commentary" regarding Edward de Vere's true right to the Bardic title. Also at this site is a beginner's guide to the Shakespeare authorship problem. But let us go on and not get tangled in such a debate.

Another top Shakespeare Internet site is the Shakespeare Web site (*www.shakespeare.com*). This is a solid site, particularly with regard to its "Queries and Replies" section about the Bard. The site also includes listings of Shakespeare theatrical productions and festivals across the country. But one gets the impression that the site hasn't been maintained much since an ambitious launch last year.

The Shakespeare Web site not only recommends MIT's Shakespeare search engine (discussed earlier), but also gives thumbs up to a search (and entire text) site maintained by James Matthew Farrow of Sydney University's Basser Department of Computer Science at *www.gh.cs. usyd.edu.au/~matty/Shakespeare/*.

The following are just a few of many helpful resources that writers can find on the Net.

- Amazon (the largest online bookseller) *www.amazon.com*
- BookMarket Update *http://bookmarket.com*
- Bookwire (top publishing industry Web site) *www.bookwire.com*
- Inkspot *www.inkspot.com*
- National Writers Union *www.nwu.org/*
- Writers on the Net *www.writers.com*

CHAPTER 22

The Arts on the Net

S ay you are given to culture and like to visit the Guggenheim in New York City, or the National Gallery in Washington, or the Los Angeles Museum of Art. And when you go abroad, there are the obligatory stops at the Tate in London, and it should go without mention that in Paris, the Louvre is a must.

But what of the Warhol Museum in Pittsburgh, the Detroit Fine Arts Institute, the Sistine Chapel at the Vatican, and the great museums and galleries of Japan and Russia?

Some Fine Evening You Can See the Great Works of Art

So let's say you really can't get to any of the above that often, but some fine evening—wherever you might be on planet earth—you can pour yourself a glass of wine, strike up the *1812 Overture,* and then seamlessly surf through the online collections of the art museums and galleries around the world, great and small—and there are many of them.

When I last wrote comprehensively about museums online, over two years ago, the best starting point was the World Wide Arts Resources Web site (*http://wwar.com*) created by Markus Kruse, then the arts curator of Ohio State University. After dropping in again, this still seems the best starting point. Among other praise, the WWAR site has been called "the Yahoo of the arts world" by *Internet World* magazine.

There are literally thousands of well-organized (and searchable) links to museums and other things artistic around the globe at the WWAR Web site, including a searchable index of over two thousand artists, information about arts schools, art for sale, and a compilation of arts publications and information about the performance arts. One caveat about the World Wide Arts Resource Web site: Though well-organized, this site is comprehensive in scope, and it can often take a bit of searching to find a specific resource.

Another Web site that can act as an excellent guide to art exhibitions around the world is the museum section of the World Wide Web Virtual Library at *www.comlab.ox.ac.uk/archive/other/museums.html*. This same page can be found through the International Council of Museums (*www.icom.org/vlmp/*).

But perhaps the best place to actually start an arts jaunt through the Net is at what is considered one of the greatest art galleries of the world, the Louvre (*http://mistral.culture.fr/louvre*), which is just as striking online as it is off.

This palace-size museum is very helpfully broken down by floor, wing, and artistic area of interest. The collections of the Louvre Museum encompass arts "dating from the birth of the great civilization . . . to the Early Middle Ages to the middle of the 19 century," the Louvre Web site informs us. The holdings are divided into seven departments, including oriental antiques, Egyptian antiques, Greek, Etruscan, and Roman antiques, and from the modern period, paintings, sculpture, objets d'art, and prints and drawings. Among the Louvre's other great works, one can pay a visit to Leonardo de Vinci's *Mona Lisa.*

Next, visit the Sistine Chapel, where famous painter Michelangelo has rendered an epic rendition of humanity across the chapel's sprawling ceiling that spans from the creation of Adam to the last judgment. This particular online exhibit is hosted by the Christus Rex Web site at *www.christusrex.org/www1/sistine/O-Ceiling.html.*

Hopping over to London, the Tate Gallery (*www.tate.org.uk*) holds a superb collection of British art that ranges from Gainsborough to

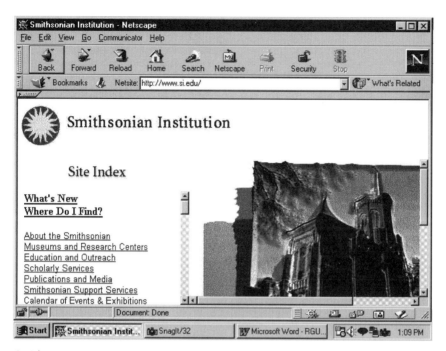

Smithsonian Institution

Reynolds, Stubbs, Blake, Palmer, and Constable, to JWM Turner. Also available is the international modern arts collection, which features important work by Picasso, Matisse, Duchamp, Mondrian, Hempworth, Magrite, Dali, Giacommetti, Dubuffet, Bacon, Pollock, Rothko, and Warhol. All in all, the Tate Web site says that it currently has over eight thousand works that can be viewed online.

Heading back across the Atlantic to Washington, D.C. (hometown to the Internet Newsroom in nearby Glen Echo, MD), visit the National Gallery of Art at *www.nga.gov/*. Here, one can find one of the finest collections of art in the world, with holdings that include major works of painting, sculpture, and the graphic arts by many notable artists. The online collection of the National Gallery can be searched by artist, title, or a combination of criteria. There are over 100,000 objects that are part of the collection that can be found at this site, according to the

National. This is one of the most elegantly designed of the various museum sites, with a simplicity of layout that nevertheless holds a great deal of material, including not only visuals, but biographical information on artists and background on the provenance of each work of art.

Also, while in Washington, a great deal of arts, educational, and historical resources can be found at the Smithsonian Institution home page. Go to *www.si.edu/*.

Coming to Netsurfers live from Pittsburgh is the Andy Warhol Museum (*www.warhol.org*), which features a tour of the facility and various works by the king of pop art, who grew up in this one-time steel town.

The famous Guggenheim Museum on Fifth Avenue in New York City is open round the clock online (*www.guggenheim.org/*), with a host of works that hail from whatever its current exhibitions are. In April 1998, the works of Frankenthaler, Rauschenberg, Iglesias, and Kelly were on view.

Next on our world cultural tour is the Detroit Institute of the Arts (*www.dia.org*), which is the fifth largest museum in the United States and boasts holdings of thousands of paintings, sculptures, graphics, and works of decorative arts.

The Los Angeles County Museum of Art (*www.lacma.org/*) is the largest art museum in western United States, with an encyclopedic collection of artistic creations that stems from prehistory to the modern era. In total, there are more that 150,000 art objects in its collection, many of which can be viewed online at the LACMA Web site. This site is also good for links to other galleries and things cultural.

Before Netsurfing across the Pacific, stop at the Fine Arts Museums of San Francisco Web site (*www.famsf.org*), which includes the De Young Museum and the Legion of Honor collection. Most rewarding of all for the online art viewer is the IMAGEBASE, which holds the images of over 65,000 works of art.

The National Museum of Japanese History (*www.rekihaku.ac.jp/*) is an excellent place to start navigating the Japanese cultural arts, including links to the Japanese Museum of Modern Art and the Kyoto National Museum.

In Russia, the Hermitage is one of the top artistic institutions to visit online (*www.hermitage.org/*), or offline, for that matter. Started by Catherine II in 1764 with her purchase of over two hundred Flemish and Dutch paintings, the collective holdings of the Hermitage Museum now includes hundreds of thousands of paintings, drawings, sculptures, historical artifacts, and other objects.

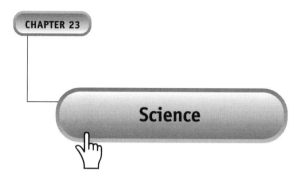

CHAPTER 23

Science

In 1980, scientists and engineers had only limited access to the highest levels of computational power. Today, they employ desktop systems of comparable power and have access through the Internet to a collection of supercomputing facilities with capabilities they could only dream about a decade ago.

Over this same period, the number of host computers on what is now the Internet has leapt from about 200 to over 10 million in 1996—a 50,000-fold increase.

—Member of the National Science Foundation speaking before the U.S. Congress. Found at *www.senate.gov/ ~commerce/hearings/bordogna.htm*

During the nineties, the Internet has expanded markedly as a method of research for things outside the sciences. Because of this, it is no longer common knowledge that the Internet and its predecessor, the National Science Foundation Net, and the ARPANet before that, were created for the exclusive use of scientific and academic researchers.

When the early Net was created in the 1960s, who would have

thought that one could research a car purchase online, or browse the Net for theater show times, or look at art online. But these things are what most people think of most often when they think of the Net.

The global Net, however, still enjoys a great volume of usage for scientific research purposes—whether it's going online to use a supercomputer at a scientific facility other than your own, or to share information and resources with fellow scientists. Perhaps of equal usefulness—and profound future implications—is the use of the Net to teach science to students of all ages.

The National Aeronautics and Space Administration (NASA) is a perfect example of how scientist, students, and the average person can use the Net. Below, I review a variety of NASA Web sites that can help you keep up with the sun, moon, and planets, as well as the new international space station.

Using Cyberspace to Explore Outer Space

The International Space Station is now under construction above the Earth. Because of this, the world's attention is drawn to the stars. But what else is happening in space? Quite a lot it seems. This may well be remembered as the golden age of robotic exploration of our solar system. Operating under the motto "smaller, faster, cheaper," the American space agency NASA is gathering scientific data at a rate that is rapidly outstripping the ability to analyze it. During the course of the next ten years, NASA is planning on sending its first craft to Pluto; sending seven robot explorers to Mars; launching a mission to sample a passing comet and return that material to Earth; and there will even be a robot probe orbiting an asteroid. For a good overview of all this planetary exploration, start at NASA's Jet Propulsion Web site at *http://pds.jpl.nasa.gov/planets*.

The Sun

The sun has been getting a lot of visitors from Earth recently, including the joint NASA–European Space Agency probe SOHO (Solar and

Space is the place as the International Space Station get assembled.

Heliopsheric Observatory), which has provided fascinating images of two "sungrazer" comets impacting on the Sun's surface. For an overview of this and other solar missions, go to *http://umbra.nascome.nasa.gov/ solar_missions.html.*

Mercury and Venus

Observed by the 1974 *Mariner 10* probe, Mercury will be getting a new visit from the European Space Agency, in a mission planned for 2005. Mercury's neighbor, Venus, was imaged by *Mariner* on its way to Mercury, and more secrets were revealed to the *Pioneer* probe in 1980. Venus was most recently surveyed by the *Magellan* spacecraft, which radar-mapped 98 percent of its surface. Mercury and Venus are explored at *http://nssdc.gsfc.nasa.gov/planetary/planets/mercurypage.html.* The *Magellan* mission to Venus can be found at *www-b.jpl.nasa.gov/ magellan/mgn.html.*

Earth and Moon

Manned space research has taken a backseat to unmanned probes since the Moon landings, but that is changing. The International Space Station had its first component launched from Kazakhstan in late 1998 and has been undergoing construction and expansion since.

Manned space exploration and work got a boost (so to speak) with the repair of the Hubble Telescope by members of a NASA space shuttle crew. The International Space Station can be found on the Internet at *http://station.nasa.gov/* and the Wide-Field Planetary Camera2 Science Team (favorite Hubble images) are at *http://wfpc2.jpl.nasa.gov/~idt/ Favorite_images.html.* Check out NASA's plans for lunar exploration at *http://nssdc.gsfc.nasa.gov/planetary/lunar/apollo_25th.html.*

Mars

While the worldwide public interest surrounding the Mars Pathfinder mission in 1997 has, of course, subsided because of the end of the mission, there is still much going on with Mars exploration.

The *Mars Global Surveyor* spacecract has been busily snapping photos of the red planet and, as of 1999, has begun begin mapping the surface of the planet. Starting in 1998 and culminating in 2005 (*Mars Sample Return* craft), there will be one Mars mission launched each year by NASA. Go to *http://mars.jpl.nasa.gov/.*

Asteroids and Comets

The movies *Deep Impact* and *Armageddon* focused much attention on the potential effects of a collision between Earth and an asteroid or comet. Hype aside, human knowledge of these heavenly bodies is still rather limited. To counter this, the Near Earth Asteroid Rendezvous mission will be launched in 1999 in the hopes of greatly increasing the amount of information known about these traveling space objects. The homepage for the NEAR mission is at *http://near.jhuapl.edu.*

Jupiter

Though hamstrung by a faulty antenna, the *Galileo* spacecraft has nonetheless been relaying spectacular images. Using its functional, but slower, backup antenna, it has been transmitting images not only of Jupiter, but its moons, and along the way, an asteroid that has a moon of its own. The *Galileo* mission is at *www.jpl.nasa.gov/galileo/*. Plans are afoot to send a craft to orbit Jupiter's moon Europa. Go to *www.jpl. nasa.gov/ice_fire/europao.htm*.

Saturn

Launched in 1997, the school-bus-sized *Cassini* probe will use four gravity-assisted flybys of Earth, two of Venus, and then Jupiter to gain enough velocity to arrive at Saturn in 2004. In addition to studying Saturn, it will drop a probe on Titan, a moon of Saturn, to study its atmosphere. Learn more about *Cassini* at *www.jpl.nasa.gov/cassini/*.

Uranus and Neptune

Due to their extreme distance (Neptune is nearly 3 billion miles away), little was known about Uranus and Neptune prior to their 1979–1981 visit from *Voyager 2*. Using gravity assists from Jupiter and Saturn, *Voyager 2* allowed NASA to explore these remote planets that never could have been visited by a directly-launched spacecraft. Among the discoveries: Neptune's moon Triton showed evidence of a faint atmosphere and geyser-like eruptions of nitrogen gas.

Voyager can be found at *http://vraptor.jpl.nasa.gov*. A large collection of photos of the four gas giant planets can be found in the *Voyager* section of the NSSDC Image Catalog at *http://nssdc.gsfc.nasa.gov/imgcat/html/index/*.

Pluto and Beyond

The only planet never to have been studied by a spacecraft, Pluto will get its chance early in the next century, when the *Pluto-Kuiper Express* will explore the ninth planet and its single moon, Charon. If all goes well, the spacecraft will venture further still, to examine the belt of comets that lies outside of Pluto's orbit. Go to *www.jpl.nasa.gov/ice_fire/PFFinfo.html*.

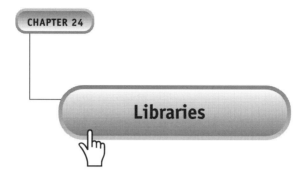

CHAPTER 24

Libraries

The Net phenomenon of school and public library online resources is a topic not sufficiently written about. One can get card catalog information, various specialized publications, and often, topically categorized compilations of Web sites that have been annotated by genuine librarians. The latter, in particular, is nothing to sneeze at (as those who have Netsurfed through the disorder of the Net for several years know), and this alone makes various library Web sites worthy places to visit. Often, these sites are an even better place to begin your broadbased Netresearch than Yahoo or certainly any of the search engines.

But first, you will want to use library Net pages to look up information on hard-copy holdings that the library may have. This is extremely valuable in that there is still quite a bit of information that is not digitized and online.

If you are researching anything ranging from Paleolithic art to classical architecture to the U.S. Civil War, you may want to use the Net to look through the catalog of your local, regional, or nearby university library, and then go check out the relevant items at the library itself.

The famous Library of Congress, headquartered on Capitol Hill, Washington, D.C., can be found online at *www.loc.gov*. You can also find the National Library of Medicine at *www.nlm.nih.gov*. The American Library Association (with extensive links to various libraries) can be found on the Web at *www.ala.org/*.

The following is a list of library Web sites, including various university and most state system libraries.

Top University Libraries

- Bucknell *http://jade.bucknell.edu/*
- Case Western *www.cwru.edu/uclibraries.html*
- Dartmouth *www.dartmouth.edu/~library*
- Duke *www.lib.duke.edu/*
- Franklin & Marshall *www.library.fandm.edu*
- Gettysburg College *www.gettysburg.edu/library/*
- Harvard *www.harvard.edu/museums/*
- Iowa State University *www.lib.iastate.edu/*
- Marquette *www.marquette.edu/library*
- Ohio State *www.lib.ohio-state.edu/*
- Penn State *www.libraries.psu.edu/*
- Princeton *http://infoshare1.princeton.edu/*
- Stanford *www-sul.stanford.edu*
- UCLA *www.library.ucla.edu*
- University of Michigan *www.library.umich.edu*
- University of Wisconsin *www.library.wisc.edu/*
- Wellesley College *http://luna.wellesly.edu/*
- Yale *www.library.yale.edu*

State Libraries

- Access Colorado Library and Information Network *www.aclin.org*
- Alaska Division of Libraries *www.educ.state.ak.us/lam/*
- Arizona Department of Library, Archives and Public Records *www.dlapr.lib.az.us/*
- California State Library *www.library.ca.gov/*
- Connecticut State Library *www.ctstateu.edu/csl/csl_home.html*
- Delaware Division of Libraries *www.lib.de.us/*

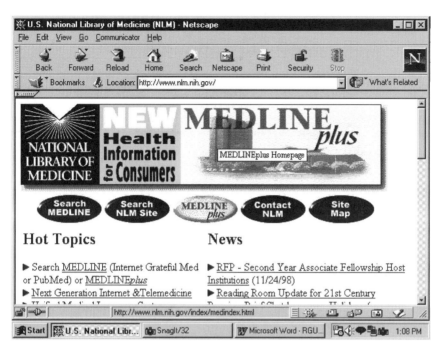

The National Library of Medicine is a top research Web site.

- Georgia Public Library Services *www.gpls.public.lib.ga.us/*
- Idaho State Library *www.isu.edu/departments/library/help.htm*
- Illinois State Library *www.sos.state.il.us/depts/library/isl_home. html*
- Indiana State Library *www.statelib.lib.in.us/*
- Kansas State Library *www.lib.ukans.edu/*
- Kentucky Department for Libraries and Archives *www.kdla.state. ky.us/*
- Library of Michigan *www.libofmich.lib.mi.us/*
- Library of Virginia *www.vsla.edu/*
- Maine State Library *www.state.me.us/msl/mslhome.htm*
- Massachusetts Library and Information Network *www.mlin.lib. ma.us/*
- Maryland Public Libraries and Online Public Information Network *http://sailor.lib.md.us*

- Mississippi Library Commission *www.mlc.lib.ms.us/*
- Missouri State Library *http://mosl.sos.state.mo.us/*
- Montana State Library *http://msl.mt.gov/*
- Nebraska Library Commission *www.nlc.state.ne.us/*
- Nevada State Library and Archives *www.clan.lib.nv.us/*
- New Hampshire State Library *www.state.nh.us/nhsl/nhsl.html*
- New Jersey State Library *www.state.nj.us/statelibrary/njlib.htm*
- New Mexico State Library *www.stlib.state.nm.us/*
- New York State Library *www.nypl.org/*
- North Dakota State Library *www.sendit.nodak.edu/ndsl/index.html*
- Oklahoma Department of Libraries *www.state.ok.us/~odl/*
- Rhode Island Office of Library and Information Services *www.dsls.state.ri.us/*
- South Carolina State Library *www.state.sc.us/scsl/*
- South Dakota State Library *www.state.sd.us/state/executive/deca/st_lib/st_lib.htm*
- State Library of Iowa *www.silo.lib.ia.us/*
- State Library of Louisiana *http://smt.state.lib.la.us/statelib.htm*
- State Library of North Carolina *http://statelibrary.dcr.state.nc.us/ncslhome. htm*
- State Library of Ohio *http://winslo.ohio.gov/*
- Tennessee State Library and Archive *www.state.tn.us/sos/statelib/tslahome.htm*
- Texas State Library and Archives Commission *www.tsl.state.tx.us/*
- Utah State Archives *www.archives.state.ut.us/*
- Utah State Library *www.state.lib.ut.us/*
- Vermont Department of Libraries *http://dol.state.vt.us/*
- Washington State Library *http://griffin/wsu.edu/*
- West Virginia Library Commission *www.wvlc.wvnet.edu/*
- Wisconsin Division for Libraries and Community Learning *http://badger.state.wi.us/agencies/dpi/dlcl/*
- Wyoming State Library *www-wsl.state.wy.us/*

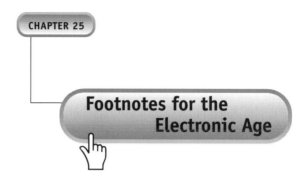

CHAPTER 25

Footnotes for the Electronic Age

Perhaps the most serious responsibility of doing research is crediting those ideas that are not one's own. Students and journalists alike are constantly reminded of the consequences of not properly crediting one's research, and several style manuals exist to help scholars record their citations uniformly and accurately. This responsibility can be characterized in the form of the Chinese proverb that asks, "If a tree falls in the forest, and no one is there to hear it, does it make any sound?" Similarly, if a journalist or scholar can't physically produce their research, how does one know it ever existed?

The wealth of electronic information has posed a two-fold problem: how to cite the information, and how to retrieve the information later when Internet addresses and Web sites are constantly changing. Most traditional citation formats include the title, author, publication, and date, as well as the page number. This information allows future researchers to go back and retrieve and/or verify the citation. With electronic information, however, page numbers are almost nonexistent. Publication dates (in the form of time/date stamps on a home page) are more common, but with the constant weeding and updating of Web information, what is accessed today may be gone tomorrow.

The standard style guides, including Turabian and MLA (see complete citation below), have taken a stab at creating standards for citing electronic resources, and a few scholars have published their own style guides on the Internet. All of these style guides vary in their treatment of electronic information. Turabian's guide, for example, includes the date the information was accessed on the Internet (by the person writing the citation), while Janice Walker's guide, published on the Internet, includes the date information was published (by the site).

As always, the best strategy in citing sources is to pick one method and be consistent. If there is a specific method already being used by your colleagues, use that method. Another tip is to print a copy of the research you gather from the Internet with a time/date stamp, which can be used later if you need it.

Here is a bibliography of relevant citation resources that can be found in print or on the Internet:

- Li, Xia and Nancy Crane. *The Official Internet World Guide to Electronic Styles: A Handbook to Citing Electronic Information.* Westport: Meckler Media, 1996. Various citation examples from the book can be found here: *www.uvm.edu/~ncrane/estyles/*
- Gibaldi, Joseph. *MLA Handbook for Writers of Research Papers.* New York: Modern Language Association of America, 1995.
- Turabian, Kate L. *A Manual for Writers of Term Papers, Theses, and Dissertations.* Chicago: University of Chicago Press, 1996.
- Walker, Janice. *MLA-Style Citations of Electronic Sources.* (*www.columbia.edu/cu/cup/cgos/*)

SECTION V

Specialized Research

CHAPTER 26

The Online Way to Finding Your Way There: Maps

There are a number of locales on the Internet which give map information for locales off the Net (i.e., the "real world") and can prove of great assistance in short or long travel planning, giving directions, and locating residences or business. The latter two functions are crucial ones to those who consider themselves information professionals. So following is a look at some of the top map spots on the Net. All are equally recommended.

Maps On Us *www.mapsonus.com*

Produced and created by Lucent Technologies (a spin-off of AT&T), the Maps On Us Web site is a good example of how these type of direction services on the Net work. And all the basic functions that we list here can be found on the other top map Web sites as well.

The easily read maps produced by the Maps On Us site can be tweaked by zooming in or out, and by panning north, south, east, or west. I have found these functions to be very handy. Depending on the level of detail you require, each street is named, and geographical details such as rivers, lakes, and small islands also get their proper monikers.

The lookup function for Maps On Us is one found at many of the other cartographic Web sites, all of which produce maps based on the address, street, county, and state information that a user puts in. From this basic level of functionality, one can get more elaborate by putting in two addresses in order to get a point-to-point map of directions.

A variation on this would be that of the business traveler who may put in the address of an office he or she will be visiting or hotel he or she is staying at in order to find out about nearby restaurants or other entertainment. When one clicks on the name of a restaurant, full yellow pages information will be listed that includes the address and phone number of the establishment and often additional information, such as menu selections or whether the establishment has a catering facility.

In this same vein, for the person doing route planning, the Maps On Us site can list many categories of business, eateries, or cultural places that may be along the route of travel. Once you have devised a map to your requirements, it can be printed out, saved, or even e-mailed to an associate in order to direct them to a particular locale. This particular function is one that I have found very handy when throwing social engagements for which a number of guests need directions. Also worth mentioning is the "text to speech" processing that allows one to hear directions to a locale if they so desire.

While Maps On Us is free and requires no registration, for those who do register, this Web site will keep a list of your map preferences (such as type of labels and so forth) and will also retain a record of the top one hundred locales that you wish to archive.

MapQuest *www.mapquest.com*

The MapQuest Web site operates in much the same way as the Maps On Us site, including the features of travel planning (with step-by-step directions if necessary) and breakout information on lodging, dining, and other attractions that might be near your route of travel. Included within this particular function is detailed city information and weather reports. Also, there is an itinerary-building function that allows you to plan your trip with almost military efficiency.

MapQuest has an alliance with City.Net (part of the Excite search engine), so you will see MapQuest in action there as well. I recommend MapQuest with as much enthusiasm as I do Maps On Us.

MapBlast *www.mapblast.com/*

And last, but not least, is MapBlast, by the Vicinity Corporation (also highly recommended). Like the other map sites, this one is meant to act as a technology showcase for its manufacturer, and is therefore free. Also similar to the other Web sites, this one allows the user to create, customize, and save easily read digital maps. Maps are generated by putting in addresses, with detailed road maps limited to just the United States for now. This is true of the other sites as well.

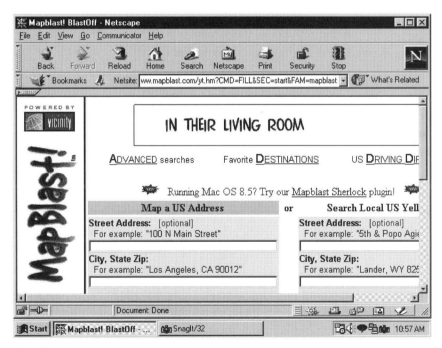

MapBlast

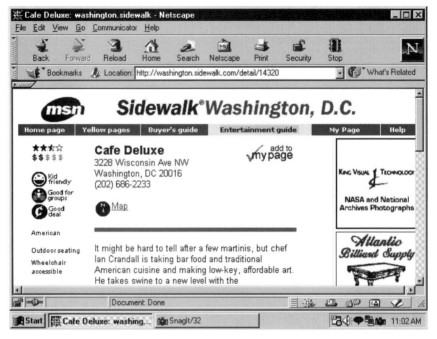

Looking for the perfect martini in Washington, D.C.?

Finding Your Way Through the Big Cities

The proliferation of city guides on the World Wide Web provides dramatic evidence of just how local the global Internet is becoming. Both the number and quality of the various city guides has increased markedly over the previous two years. The city guides include simple sets of links for a specific city, such as City.Net and Cityguide, which are hosted by the Excite and Lycos search engines, respectively; and the more formal guides such as CitySearch or Sidewalk, which have their own writers churning out local copy on where to go and what to do.

There has been much talk in the print media, such as newspapers and city magazines, about the competitive threat posed by these new virtual city guides. The fear is that consumers will turn to the new media for the local information franchise long held in monopoly by the print media, and once that happens, advertising revenue will follow.

A good look at Sidewalk, which is a city guide recently launched by

Microsoft's Sidewalk, indicates that the traditional print and electronic media have reason to be worried. Though only available for a handful of cities now, Sidewalk has announced plans to launch editions in fifty cities soon, with comprehensive local listings.

Sidewalk *www.sidewalk.com/*

At its most basic level, Sidewalk offers the kind of restaurant, club, theater, sports, and other local listings that the metro newspapers and magazines have done for years, in small type near the back or in special sections. With Sidewalk (as with all things online, including the digital editions of newspapers), these listings are highly searchable.

"Sidewalk will be produced by local editorial teams that include print, broadcast, and online journalists who will work together to deliver on our promise of providing the next generation of city media," said Frank Schott, Sidewalk publisher, at the launch of his city guide. Heading Sidewalk's Washington office is Anne Karalekas, former director of marketing for the *Washington Post* and publisher of that newspaper's weekly magazine section. So it's easy to see the competition that Sidewalk creates for the average big metro daily.

Looking for Mexican, or shall we say sushi, tonight in the nation's capitol? Well, look no further than either Microsoft's Washington Sidewalk (*http://washington.sidewalk.com/*) or Washington Post.com (*www.washingtonpost.com/*). Both will give you the name, address, and telephone numbers of relevant eateries in town, including notes on the quality of the cuisine. The same goes for club, theater, sports, and other allied establishments.

But, say you are traveling from Washington to Seattle. Well, you're not going to get the name of a good martini lounge in Seattle from Washington Post.com, are you? You will, however, get a good Seattle martini lounge from Seattle Sidewalk, at *http://seattle.sidewalk.com.*

This is not to tout Microsoft as a local information provider, but rather to point out the obvious difference in having a centralized resource for city information. The Sidewalk city listings thus far include Boston, New York, San Diego, San Francisco, the Twin Cities, and Sydney,

Australia. Also, the service has content relationships with the *Seattle Times* and the *Village Voice*.

CitySearch.com *www.citysearch.com/*

Garnering as much attention as Sidewalk is the Pasadena-based City-Search Web site, which, much like Sidewalk, has built itself from the ground up in a number of cities, towns, and communities by forging relationships with local businesses, civic groups, and educational institutions.

Given an "Editor's Choice Award" by *PC Magazine* as the top Web Regional Guide, the CitySearch site proclaims itself as "a complete and current community guide, delivering up-to-date information on arts and entertainment events, community activities and local businesses to consumers via the Internet."

Cities that it covers currently include New York, San Francisco, Austin, Salt Lake City, Nashville, Portland, Raleigh-Durham/Chapel Hill, Pasadena, and Melbourne, Australia. CitySearch has media content partnerships with Time Out New York, the Washington Post, and local affiliates of ABC, CBS, and Fox. And it maintains strategic informational partnerships with Ticketmaster and BellSouth.Net.

Newspapers

The print media industry has, in part, rushed to solve some of its dilemma (i.e., having great local and regional information franchises, but no centralized entrance door for all these localized listings) by launching a variety of city guide efforts.

Knight-Ridder, for instance, has been rolling out local entertainment guides online as part of its New Media Real Cities network (*www.justgo. com/*). The guides have been appearing under the JustGo logo, which includes five cities thus far, Detroit being the most recent. Offerings in JustGo range from restaurant reviews to arts, entertainment, and movie listings.

More City Guides

Other city guides are provided by America Online and the search engines Excite and Lycos. America Online, the eight-hundred-pound guerrilla of the online world (with over 10 million subscribers), began rolling out its Digital City guides (*www.digitalcity.com*) over two years ago with offerings that include local movie, dining, and real estate guides and a classifieds section.

Digital City straddles the members-only AOL and the Web, with the Web section encompassing almost twenty-five cities, including Boston, New York, Philadelphia, Pittsburgh, Washington, Detroit, Dallas, Phoenix, Las Vegas, Los Angeles, and San Francisco.

Both of the well-regarded search engines Excite and Lycos have played host to municipal guides for several years now, essentially by compiling relevant links for any given city across the globe. These include local newspapers, TV, and radio, along with local organizations, business, and entertainment. For the Excite City.Net, check out *www. city.Net/*. For the Lycos Cityguide, go to *http://cityguide.lycos.com/*.

CHAPTER 27

Finding People: Where Are They Now?

If asked several years ago how to find someone's e-mail address, I would have told you, "Call them on the phone for their electronic mail address; it's quicker."

But not today. While there is no single online directory that lists all 100 million estimated Netusers, it's not as true anymore that you can't find someone's e-mail address via the Net. To do so, there are a number of services that use simple name keyword searches, with most also providing for advanced queries.

Following is a rundown of some of the top "people finder" engines currently available on the Net:

Four11 *www.Four11.com*

Founded in 1994, this service was one of the earliest of the people finders—thus making it one of the best by default. It has kept pace by constantly updating its database, making it an e-mail and phone number resource of continuing merit.

Among other boasts, the Four11 service has on file the entirety of the U.S. telephone white pages. As for e-mail, the current figure is above 13 million individuals' addresses. In addition to providing for searches

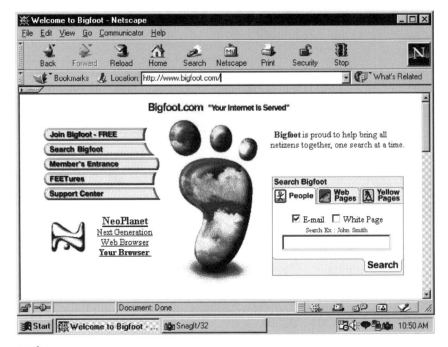

Bigfoot

for an individual's e-mail address, this service will also notify you if the address you are looking for is currently unavailable (unknown). And you can ask Four11 to advise you at a future date if the address has been added to its database.

Four11 has partnerships with the famous Yahoo information Web site and with the Infoseek search engine, so I assume that means when you use the people-find functions for those services, you are accessing the Four11 database.

Bigfoot *www.bigfoot.com*

Also an early presence in the Internet people-finding business was Bigfoot, which was founded in 1995 and, like Four11, lays claim to having the largest database of e-mail addresses available. The Bigfoot service also has the entire U.S. white pages. Bigfoot says that it has "the most accurate list of names and addresses on the Internet."

Among other interesting features is that, if an individual user would like, Bigfoot will submit a "Do Not Mail" request on your behalf to Net marketers. Whether spammers honor this request is as yet in question, but I am looking into it.

WhoWhere *www.whowhere.com/*

The WhoWhere people finding service also maintains a large e-mail database with more than 11 million e-mail addresses available. And like the other services, it allows for white-page types of phone and home address searches, through 90 million U.S. residential listings.

But wait, that's not all. WhoWhere has business yellow pages with the numbers and locales of 14 million U.S. businesses. Also, in a "community building" effort, WhoWhere boasts an "affinity interest search." With this type of search function, one can find people with interests similar to one's own, or at least persons who have an interest in a topic one may be researching.

Four11 has a similar search function that allows one to search by "interest" and by "past high school," "past college," "past military," and so on.

Internet@ddress.Finder *www.iaf.net*

This service functions the same as those listed earlier, allowing for searches by last name, first name, organization, and Net domain. Also, one can put in an e-mail address, and it will match that address to a name.

The search capability of Internet@ddress.Finder is somewhat limited, because there are under 6 million listings currently available. Still, one might give the service a shot, because some person's e-mail may be listed here and not with one of the larger services.

Search Engines

In addition to their main function of looking for topical material, a number of the Internet search engines also boast people-finding capability. I found these to be at least as accurate as some of the services mentioned above.

As mentioned earlier, some engines have partnerships with these services. The Excite search engine is in partnership with WhoWhere. WhoWhere is also hosted by the Lycos search engine at *www.lycos.com*.

CHAPTER 28

Customized Home Pages: Getting Personal

Tired of getting the same old impersonal screen when your default home page loads on your Web browser? Now, with very little effort, you can get an opening screen that contains exactly the kind of individualized content you have requested.

The concept is called "personalization" and it is certain to become highly popular as more Internet users learn about it and discover how to harness the service.

Among those with popular personalization services are Netscape Communicator (*http://my.netscape.com*), Yahoo (*http://my.yahoo.com*), and the search engines Excite (*www.excite.com*) and Lycos (*http://personal.lycos.com*). Microsoft's Internal Explorer (*http://home.microsoft.com*) is still in the early stages, with its "Start" page which users can personalize to a limited extent.

All of the personalized services basically offer the same approach; you sign up for the free service, provide a user name and password, then use a menu to select the type of content you want on your opening screen. Organizations like Excite and Yahoo, which do not have their own browsers, give you the option of making their personal page your home page.

As an example, let's look closely at two of the personalized services, the one offered by Netscape and Excite's service, and briefly examine Yahoo and Lycos programs.

Netscape, still the most popular browser, has an icon labeled "My Netscape" on its home page which takes you to the personalizing section. A "Help" menu walks you through the process, which first involves entering a user name and password, then the selection of content you desire on the personalized page. You have your choice of news headlines that will be displayed: top stories, business news, sports, entertainment, and so on. Then you choose stock market information, requesting quotes on your own portfolio or simply on the Dow Jones and NASDAQ indicators. You can also request a horoscope, weather report, and other specialized info.

The Excite personal service is somewhat similar. It will give you current stock quotes, the weather forecast of your particular area, and all kinds of news headlines.

Both Netscape and Excite offer users the opportunity to make changes in content and to tweak the layout and colors of their new personalized pages. Yahoo, the granddaddy of Internet directories, also offers a well-regarded personalization service.

A caveat: the questionnaire used to determine content on the Yahoo personal page is much longer than those on Netscape and Excite and as a result the amount of data returned on the personal page can be overwhelming.

The Lycos personalization service is reached by clicking on the "Personal Guide" label on the main Lycos page. A help section easily walks you through the process of creating a personal page.

These new personalized pages follow an earlier Internet fad which used so-called "push" technology. Push technology meant that companies like Web broadcaster Pointcast would automatically send and update large amounts of information to subscribers' hard drives (as opposed the subscriber going to the site and retrieving the files). The push approach fell out of favor because it provided more information than subscribers wanted.

The reason companies like Netscape, Yahoo, and Excite have quickly embraced the personalization technique is two-fold. First, they hope the service will make them more popular and generate more visitors. And, secondly, they believe it will help them sell more advertising on their sites because they will be delivering a targeted audience.

APPENDIX A

Getting Connected:
Some Net Basics

I t's easy to get connected to the Internet—a simple telephone call will get you online—but it's difficult deciding what kind of a connection is best for you. There are literally hundreds of local, regional, and national companies willing to sign you up to the Internet for a fee. It's as if you had to choose between more than two thousand phone companies when you moved to a new community and were putting in telephone service for the first time.

There are several simple guideposts you can follow to make the decision easy. If you are brand new to the Internet, the best course is to sign up with one of the big commercial online services. They make the process simple, provide lots of help to novice Netsurfers, and throw in vast amounts of informative and entertaining content from their own resources.

If you are already comfortable with the Internet, as a result of college experience or a workplace connection, you will probably want to sign up with an Internet service provider (ISP), where you will get competitive rates and reliable service.

There are local, regional, and national Internet service providers. All will hook you up to the Internet, but the quality of the service and the customer support varies widely.

Choosing an ISP

As 1998 drew to a close there were nearly 5,500 Internet service providers prepared to connect you to the Internet for a fee. So how to you select an ISP if you are new to the Internet? Which ones provide good and reliable service, and which ones do a poor job?

There are several ways to find out. First, check with friends and business acquaintances in your community to find out what ISPs they use. Then check the Yellow Pages and make some phone calls to find out about rates and services of local ISPs. Various disinterested organizations provide ISP ratings that are useful to consumers, and these can be found in the Internet books that line the shelves of your local library.

You can also get reliable information about ISPs on the Internet itself. The largest collection of ISPs is at a site called "The List" sponsored by the Mecklermedia publishing company. At the end of 1998 it listed nearly 5,400 and provided a search mechanism to help find those in your community. Each listing includes information about rates and services, and some are reviewed. Address of The List is *http://thelist. internet.com.*

Periodically, the Internet magazine *CNet* (*www.cnet.com*) rates ISPs and reviews some of them. The latest (December 1998) *CNet* rundown selected four national ISPs as noteworthy, and another four as "up and comers."

The Big Four named by *CNet* were:

- America Online, priced at $21.95 monthly for unlimited service, and offering 100 free hours to new subscribers. It was *CNet's* "Editors Choice" as the best of the biggies. 800-827-6364.
- AT&T WorldNet, priced at $19.65 monthly for 150 hours and 99-cents for each additional hour. 800-967-5363.
- CompuServe, priced at $24.94 monthly for unlimited access, 30-day free trial, was acquired by AOL but retains an independent identity. 800-848-8990.
- MSN Internet Access, priced at $19.95 monthly for unlimited access, offers a 30-day free trial. 800-386-5550.

The four smaller, but reliable, ISPs named by CNet, were:

- EarthLink, priced at $19.95 monthly for unlimited use. 800-395-8425.
- GTE, priced at $19.95 monthly for 100 hours plus $1 for each additional hour. 888-483-6381.
- MindSpring, priced at $19.95 monthly for unlimited use. 888-677-7464.
- Netcom, priced at $19.95 monthly for unlimited use.800-638-2661.

There are certain things you should find out before signing up with an ISP. First, can you reach them and connect to the Internet with a local phone call? If not, you will run up big phone bills when you are Netsurfing. Most of the national ISPs have hundreds of so-called "Points of Presence," or local phone numbers. Also make sure they support fast modem speeds or you will be waiting forever for pages to load. They should support 56K modems. Also find out about technical service; is there someone available around the clock to answer your questions?

Hardware

Almost any up-to-date computer and modem can be used to connect to the Internet. But, as in all things in the computer world, bigger and faster is better.

A bare-bones rig that will enable you to use the Internet and the graphics-rich World Wide Web to gather information, contact sources, and tap into government data should include the following: a computer with at least a 486 chip, a 250 to 500 megabyte hard disk, 8 megabytes of memory (RAM), a 14,400 baud (or bits per second) modem, and a Web browser such as Netscape Navigator or Microsoft Explorer. That's enough to let you surf around the Internet, gather information, send and receive e-mail, and plug into Usenet newsgroups.

But the above represents the absolute minimum.

To use Windows 95, you will need a more powerful rig, of course. The 486 chip will do the job, but a Pentium would be best, along with

16 or 32 RAM of memory and a bigger hard disk, which will allow you to store more Internet material. And a 56 bps modem.

A stripped-down system will get you on the Net, but like a 1960 VW Beetle, an underpowered system will leave you hugging the right-hand shoulder of the information superhighway. Most new computers purchased today will come equipped with everything you need to venture into cyberspace in style.

Consumer's Guide to Providers

The Internet's soaring popularity for conducting research, making contacts, conducting interviews, and exchanging e-mail makes an Internet connection almost mandatory these days, especially in a metropolitan area. But how do you choose from the multitude of providers? There are several questions you should ask any potential Internet access provider before you write that check, according to respected providers we have interviewed.

Question One: Who Answers the Phone?

The most important item in determining the worth of a provider is whether or not there is someone available to take your calls during business hours. Services run by answering machine indicate that the business may be a sideline for the owner, which does not bode well for the new user or those with questions or complaints that must be addressed quickly. Long waits or needing to leave messages because no one is available are also bad signs if they occur regularly. Your provider should also be within your local dialing area.

Question Two: What Services are Offered?

At the very least, you should demand the following services from any provider: electronic mail, Usenet discussion groups, FTP, Telnet, Gopher, access to the World Wide Web, plus the ability to upload and download files from your home computer. You should also find out how much space your account includes for storing files on the server; 5MB is the most common limit; 2MB is probably not enough, especially if you are going to put your own home page on the Web.

Question Three: How Many Phone Lines are Available?

One of the most common complaints from Internet account holders are the constant busy signals that plague some providers. Find out the ratio of users to phone lines for each company; 8 to 1 is good, while ratios above 12 to 1 greatly reduce your chance of reliably finding an open line. Also, make sure the provider can support at least 28.8K bps modems.

Question Four: How Is the Provider Connected to the Internet?

If system performance is a concern, make sure the provider has at least a 256K bps connection, with either a T1 or T3 line preferred. Also, ask what kind of workstation the company uses as its primary server. If it's a PC, you might want to look elsewhere, as the smaller personal systems can be overwhelmed by loads that are handled easily by the more powerful SparcStation 10's, SparcStation 20's, and HP server line.

Question Five: Is Live Technical Support Available, at Least During Business Hours?

A corollary to Question One is the willingness of your provider to help you through the problems you encounter while using their service. You should certainly purchase a basic Internet reference work (check out *The Whole Internet User's Guide and Catalog*, second edition, by Ed Krol and Mike Loukides, published by O'Reilly and Associates, 1994), but a provider's willingness to make someone available to answer your questions, handle your comments or complaints, and steady your nerves is a major plus.

Question Six: What Do You Do to Protect My Privacy?

No system administrator worthy of the name would leave a system open to hackers, but even the most clever techniques can be defeated by a determined attacker. Ensure that your provider does not leave sensitive personal information (such as credit card numbers, phone numbers, or addresses) on the system where they could be discovered. You might also inquire whether the company sells its mailing list to information brokers and what steps need to be taken so that your entry is excluded from the list if you so desire.

Question Seven: How Much Does All This Cost?
Assuming that the provider has answered all of your questions satisfactorily, make sure that the price is both reasonable and predictable (no hidden charges). Look for the following items:
- Flat rate, unlimited-time access. Most providers allow their users to stay online as long as they care to with no hourly charge, although if the amount of time included per day is sufficient (at least four hours), this requirement may be modified. In the Washington, D.C., area, $20 per month is average for an unlimited-time account, though you can often get discounts by signing up for a year at a time.
- No start-up fee.
- No surcharge for using particular services, especially electronic mail or the World Wide Web.
- A refund or cancellation policy should you move or decide to discontinue your business with this provider.
- A written contract with a system use policy and charging plan explained in plain language.

If all of these questions can be answered to your satisfaction, ask for a trial period of not less than five days so you can test and evaluate the system. If it works as expected, you have probably found the provider for you. Of course, you should stay in touch with the provider to let them know if they are falling short of your expectations or if they are continuing to provide good access and support.

An ISDN Connection

If you want to go first-class, you can connect to the Internet through an Integrated Services Digital Network, or ISDN for short. Essentially, it's a souped up telephone line (digital versus analog) which allows Internet connections at about four times the speed of the fast 28.8K bps modems.

An ISDN line is ordered from your local telephone company, and such service was available in about 70 percent of the country by the end of 1996. The cost averages $30 per month. There is also a modest cents-per-minute fee charged for actual usage, like making a long distance call.

If you invest in an ISDN line, you still need an Internet provider who has the technology to handle such a high-speed hookup. You also need several special pieces of hardware attached to your computer that take the place of your modem. For this, you get blazing speed on the Internet. No long waits for graphics-rich pages to load. Swift downloads of data. Be warned, however, that ISDN lines are very difficult to setup and configure.

The Internet on TV

A new generation of electronic devices enable users to Netsurf on their living room television sets. They are small boxes which rest atop the TV set, cost about $300, and are sold in electronics stores.

For about $20 per month, the set-top Internet box gives you unlimited time on the Internet, with a wireless keyboard used to navigate and the results displayed on the TV set. The actual Internet connection is made with a modem built into the box and hooked to your family phone line. Initial reviews of this "Web TV" setup have been positive.

A Cable Modem

Now that we have informed you of the availability and the speed of ISDN lines, you should also be informed that ISDNs and other slower types of connections may become obsolete within a few years because of incredibly fast cable modems.

These hookups to the Net promise to deliver the full science fiction-like effect of cyberspace that is often written about when one reads about the "information superhighway." For starters, you will be able to get real time video feeds over the Net, and thereby order movies from vast data banks. In addition, cable modems will herald the beginning of the first interactive television. But the possibilities aren't limited to just the parochial purpose of watching movies and interactive TV over the Net. Everything that is accessible over the Internet will be delivered all the faster.

The cable modems currently undergoing testing operate up to 1,000 times faster than a 14,400 bps modem. Under regular modem speed, for instance, it takes around 18 hours to download Windows 95 software via the Internet, but with a cable modem, this could be done in about a minute. Several commercial organizations—including Tell-Communications Inc., Time Warner, Comcast, and Continental Cablevision—began offering cable modems in a few markets during 1996, but their plans aren't yet set in stone. And it will be a while yet until this type of hookups are available across the country.

Navigating the Net: A Guide to Understanding URLs

For those just entering cyberspace, the lengthy Net site addresses that are used can seem a touch confusing. Those addresses, by the way, are called URLs, for "uniform resource locators." You may ask, Why are they so long? Why are some longer than others? But once you understand how to read and use addresses—URLs in particular—you will be able to navigate the Internet with relative ease and speed.

Any Internet address is comprised of several components. For URLs, the part that comes after the *http://* consists of the host name, the directory path, and a file name. Remember, anything with the prefix http, means that a particular site is located on a World Wide Web server. Here's the URL for the home page of the *Internet Newsroom,* my monthly newsletter publication: *http://www.editors-service.com/articles/art98. html.*

The */www.editors-service.com/* is the host name, and the */articles/* section is the directory path, and *art98.html* is the file name.

Many lengthy addresses you will encounter appear as such because they have a long set of "subpaths" after the original directory path. Here's an example of how to reach the opening lines of *Hamlet* on the Internet, which involves several subpaths: *http://www.mindspring.com/ ~hamlet/hamlet/hamlet11.html.*

The */~hamlet/* is the directory path, and then all the "hamlets" after that are subpaths to the opening lines.

Gopher addresses can also be expressed in URL form, as appears below for the National Institutes of Health: *gopher://gopher.nih.gov/*.

In standard Gopherspace (off the Web) you would just type in this address: *gopher.nih.gov/*, without the *gopher://* part.

The same goes for FTP, which can be used as a URL by typing *ftp://* and then the address.

Browsers

To understand the sudden explosion of the Internet and the rapid growth of the Net's most popular part—the World Wide Web—it's necessary to understand the history of Mosaic, the first Web "browser" to come into use.

A browser allows an Internet user to easily access and download the informative multimedia documents available on the World Wide Web. The Web was created in 1991 by scientists at the European Particle Physics Laboratory (CERN, in its French acronym), and its emergence changed everything. The Web and the invention of Mosaic as a browser made the previously unwieldy Internet easy to use. Previously on the Internet, the only way to navigate this global computer network was using Unix commands and sifting through rather unattractive text interfaces. While this text-based interface is often still the faster method of traveling on the Net, the Web has made the Internet easy to use and attractive. With browsing software such as Mosaic or Netscape, all a Net navigator need do is point and click their mouse onto a "highlighted" or underlined word (a text or "hypertext" link), which then connects to a "document" which can contain text, graphics, video, and even sound.

This was all made possible because, in the search for making the Internet easier, the CERN programmers created a standard for data and a universal addressing system that led not only to an explosion of Internet usage, but also to a huge push toward publishing material of all types on the Internet. Using commands that are relatively simple, anyone—a company, college, government agency, or indeed, a newspaper—can publish material in hypertext, wherein certain parts of a document become a "link" to yet another document. This creates the effect from which the Web gets its name—a seamless flow of information that is intertwined. The beginning point for any Net travel and any particular site—be it corporate or otherwise—is known as a "home page," and each succeeding link leads to yet more "pages." A browser acts as reader of hypertext language.

It did take the invention of browsers such as Mosaic, as a complement to the World Wide Web, to allow for the point-and-click interface that has become so popular. Mosaic was invented at the National Center for Supercomputing Applications (NCSA) at the University of Illinois in early 1993. After a story ran in the *New York Times* about Mosaic, there were more than a thousand people a day flooding the Internet to download Mosaic software, made available free by NCSA.

While this "client" browser software—in its upgraded version—is still available via NCSA, there are also commercially licensed versions available, such as the Mosaic software sold by Spry Inc. under the name "Internet-In-A-Box." All of the World Wide Web browsers are somewhat derived from the original Mosaic software. Each of the three big commercial online services—Prodigy, America Online, and CompuServe—now use similar-looking browsers to offer Internet access to their subscribers.

The browsers all have a window that one opens to type in the address of the World Wide Web site he or she wants to reach. If you want to get to a location on the Web but don't know the address, there are search tools provided that will look it up for you. Once you find a site you like or find productive, you can add it to a "Hot List" or "Bookmark" on your browser, where it can be retrieved quickly.

Since its inception, the original Mosaic has been superseded by the Netscape Navigator, which was designed by one of the original creators of Mosaic. The Netscape Navigator, produced by Netscape Communications Corp., currently accounts for about half of the browser software used throughout the Net. Netscape used to dominate the browser market, but then software giant Microsoft entered the fray with its Internet Explorer browser, which most experts say is equal to or better than Netscape Navigator. Microsoft was so aggressive in grabbing for market share that they got slapped with a Justice Department antitrust suit which is still pending.

At my company, the Internet Newsroom, we actually use several different browsers, depending on our connection. We have connections to the Internet through several private providers and through the ubiquitous AOL company. I don't, however, recommend that everybody get that many connections.

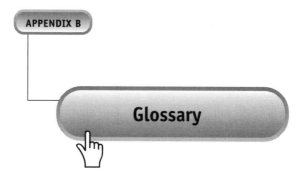

APPENDIX B

Glossary

To help the novice navigate the unfamiliar waters of the Internet, I have compiled a list of essential, informative, and amusing terms common to global networking.

Before we proceed in alphabetical order, let's start with the word "Internet."

The Internet The common name for a global collection of interlinked computer networks, all using the same communication protocol (see *TCP/IP*). Also commonly known as "the Net."

Must Know Net.Glossary

ARPANet The Internet's direct ancestor. It began operation in 1969 with money from the Defense Department's Advanced Research Projects Agency.

ASCII (American standard code information interchange) This is the de facto world-wide standard for the code numbers that are employed by computers to designate all upper and lower case latin letters, numbers, punctuations, etc. Knowing about ASCII, or at least that it exists, is handy for sending text over the Internet in some cases.

Backbone This is the high-speed line or set of connections that are the major framework for data transmission within a network. The Internet, being a network of networks, uses a variety of backbones maintained by different organizations, both academic and commercial.

Bandwidth The bandwidth of your Internet connection determines how much data can be sent over the line. Standard copper wire telephone connections are the lowest bandwidth, and fiber optics the highest. Also, the capacity to transmit or absorb information. Used to describe both computer systems and people. Low-bandwidth folks can be easily spotted by the flashing 12:00 on their VCRs.

Baud The baud rate of a modem is commonly understood to mean how many bits-per-second (bps) it can transmit.

Bit (binary digit) The bit is a single number in based-2 (binary), which means it is either a 1 or a zero. The bit is also the smallest unit of computerized data.

Byte Eight bits make up a byte's worth of data.

bps (bits-per-second) This is the measurement of data speed from one computer location to another, i.e., a 28,800 modem can move data at a rate of 28,800 bits-per-second. Also known as a baud rate.

Browser The chief "client" software used for accessing the Internet, a browser allows you to "read" the material—text, graphics—that is on the World Wide Web. Currently, the most popular browser in use is Netscape Navigator.

Client This is a software application that allows for extracting a variety of "services" for a server computer, such as having a browser, e-mail, or FTP client, each of which allow you to use these respective services from a network server computer.

Clipper chip A government-sponsored plan for telecommunications encryption. While signals would automatically be encrypted, the Feds would keep a master list of decryption keys.

Cyberspace The virtual environment that exists within a global computer network and the place where discussion, news, and events happen in the online world. Coined by William Gibson in his 1984 novel *Neuromancer*, the term has spawned new suffixes and prefixes—Cyberpunks and Gopherspace, to name a few.

DNS (domain name system) This is the distributed database system whereby domain names such as cogsum.com are translated into IP numbers or vice versa. When surfing the Net, you may occasionally receive a "DNS Error" message with regard to a Net page or document that you may be trying to access. In essence, this means that the Net address that you have been using is wrong or that this page or document has been taken offline or is temporarily inaccessible.

E-mail (electronic mail) A form of asynchronous communication on the Internet and other networks—i.e., the recipient does not have to be online at the time the message is sent. Also used as a remote information distribution system—"an e-mail server." The e-mail application was one of the first and greatest usages (in volume and usefulness) of the Internet and remains one of chief functions of the Net.

FAQ (frequently asked questions) A list of questions, posted regularly in Usenet newsgroups, in the FTP site *rfm.mit.edu*, and other Web sites that seeks to answer common questions for new members or Internet users. Reading the FAQ is a good way to avoid getting flamed.

Flame To yell at someone or otherwise criticize the person online. Flam-

ing e-mail is often distinguished by the USE OF CAPITAL LETTERS AND EX-
CLAMATION MARKS!!!

Gopher This aptly named rodent "client" utility is the best way to ne-
gotiate the Net if you have a text-based connection. It enables you to
browse through a large series of interconnected menus.

GIF (graphics interchange format) The most common type of image
file found on the Net. Limited to 256 colors, it is gradually being supplanted by the 24-bit joint photographic experts group (JPEG) compres-
sion format, which allows smaller file sizes.

Host These are the computers on the Internet that act as the reposi-
tory for services and data that can be used by other computers connecting to the host. The host computer is also where a "home page" is
geographically located.

HTTP (hypertext transport protocol or **hypertext transfer protocol)** The protocol whereby the Web works, using "hypertext" links to
connect files across the entire Internet.

ISDN (integrated services digital network) In essence, a digital phone
line (versus an analog line) that allows for much greater bandwidth and
a consequent decrease in the amount of time you spend in download-
ing documents from the Net. Bell Atlantic and other of the "Baby Bells"
are equipped to provide this type of connection to businesses and
homes, and the cost for such as connection has been decreasing.

Keyword Usually used with regard to performing a "keyword search"
while using one of the various Internet search engines. The majority
of indexing by the engines is done using keywords, so in essence, when
one is information hunting for certain subject matter (animal, vegetable,
mineral), then you use a word that is relevant to or within the subject
at hand to find a useful citation or reference upon the Net.

Mail bomb The punishment of choice for serious violators of the rules of behavior of the Usenet. A mail bomb is a huge e-mail message that clogs a perpetrator's host system. When hundreds of mail bombs deluge a system, it can cause a computer to crash. Similarly, a fax bomb sends an endless sheet of black paper to the victim's fax, consuming the paper supply or burning out the machine.

Mosaic One of the original browser software clients for navigating the World Wide Web, which can be reached via a graphics-based Internet connection. A Windows-type program, Mosaic is pretty cool looking, but has long since become outstripped by the Netscape series of browsers.

Modem Fast becoming one of the chief pieces of computer equipment of the tail end of the century, the modem is that particular computer peripheral that is used to allow a computer to connect to the phone system (or other types of data lines) and thence to other computers or computer networks, most notably the Internet. The term comes from an amalgam of the words "modulate-demodulate," which is how the modem works.

Multimedia Whether it's CD-ROMs or documents on the World Wide Web, if it combines text, pictures, sound, and video, or just any two of these "media," then it counts as multimedia.

Netscape This is currently the most popular browser software used to surf the Net and accounts for anywhere between 75 to 85 percent of browsers that are used to access the World Wide Web. It is so popular that many persons use the term Netscape in a generic sense, in the same way the trademark name Rollerblade has come to describe inline skates.

Netiquette The unofficial "rules of etiquette" on the Internet. Small violations often result in flaming, while more serious offenses risk incurring a mail bomb attack.

Net.god An old-timer in the Net.world. One who remembers when the Net was only two computers and a piece of string.

Netsurfer One who cruises the waves of the Net, perpetually looking for news spots to get their feet wet. Also, used as a term for connecting to the Net just for the thrill of exploration. Often referred to simply as "surfing."

Newbie A Net newcomer. A negative term used by old-timers who resent the use of resources by an ever-expanding population of network novices. Most common usage as in "clueless Newbie."

Packet The Internet breaks up data traveling to and from different Net sites into packets that are "bundles" of data, each assigned a numbered identity and a relevant Net address. Thus, the way the Net operates is known as "packets switching."

Server This term is used interchangeably to designate either the software that is used on one particular computer of a network that allows that computer to offer a service to another computer, such as sending a file upon command or to describe the computer upon which this server software resides. The server responds to client software in rendering a requested service.

Snail mail This derogatory term is used to describe the comparison between e-mail and traditional hard copy mail. The terms is often particularly used to single out mail that is conveyed by the U.S. Postal Service.

Spamming To send out multiple non-germane posting on the Usenet. Posting messages that have nothing to do with the affected newsgroups is a cardinal Net.sin. The response can be severe. See *Mail bomb*.

Slip/PPP (serial line Internet protocol/point-to-point protocol) One of the several methods for connecting directly to the Net over the phone.

Smiley This is the smiling face :) used as punctuation in e-mail missives. The smiley and other similar types of emotional emphasis in e-mail, such as : (, are known as "emoticons."

Telnet A way of tapping into a remote computer—as if directly connected—in order to access its publicly available files.

TCP/IP (transmission control protocol/Internet protocol) The shared language of all computers on the Net.

Timeout A timeout is when two computers that are connected over a network (such as the Internet) lose the connection because one of the computers fails to respond over a set time period.

Usenet This is the oftentimes anarchic arrangement of computer systems that exchange so-called news (individual message postings) among the newsgroups. A great deal of the Usenet intersects with the Internet-at-large.

URL (uniform resource locator) The URL of a Web site is simply its address upon the Internet. The most common protocol used in URLs is the hypertext transfer protocol (HTTP). Thus, most Net addresses start with the *http://* prefix and then continue on into the particular domain and file that you may be looking for. URLs can also be expressed as *FTP://* or as *gopher://* for Net documents that are archived within those respective protocols.

Username This is the name that you use to log into (or onto) a computer system or network (such as the Net). It is often used as your e-mail name as well.

World Wide Web (WWW) This is the most organized facet of the Net by virtue of a series of interconnected "pages" that may include text, graphics, sound, and video.

APPENDIX C

Web Sites and Internet Addresses

Note: *Web addresses beginning with both "http://" and "www" have been abbreviated to just the "www" prefix.*

The Agent Sourcebook	www.opensesame.com/agents/
AltaVista	www.altavista.digital.com/
Amazon.com	www.amazon.com
America's Job Bank	www.ajb.dni.us/
American Bar Association (ABA)	www.abanet.org
American Demographics Inc.	www.marketingtools.com
American Journalism Review	www.newslink.org
American Journalism Review's Newslink	
	http://ajr.newslink.org
American Law Sources Online	www.lawsource.com/also/
American Library Association	www.ala.org/
American Stock Exchange	www.amex.com
The Andy Warhol Museum	www.warhol.org
Anywho Directory Service	www.anywho.com
Autonomy Agentware	www.agentware.com/
Bigfoot	www.bigfoot.com
Bookwire	www.bookwire.com
BookMarket Update	http://bookmarket.com
The *Boston Globe*	www.boston.com/globe/archives
BotSpot	http://botspot.com/
Chatterbots	www.chatter-bots.com/
BullsEye Bot (Intelliseek)	www.intelliseek.com/
BusinessWire	www.businesswire.com
Cable News Network Interactive	www.cnn.com
CareerMosaic	www.careermosaic.com/
CareerPath.Com	www.careerpath.com/
Charles Schwab	www.schwab.com
Christus Rex	www.christusrex.org/
Cityguide (Lycos)	http://cityguide.lycos.com/
City.Net (Excite)	www.city.net/

CitySearch.com   www.citysearch.com/
Cnet   www.cnet.com
CNNFN   http://cnnfn.com/markets/quotes.html
College Grad Job Hunter   www.collegegrad.com
Complete Works of William Shakespeare (at the Massachusetts Institute of Technology)
                                   http://the-tech.mit.edu/Shakespeare/works.html
The Computer-Assisted Reporting page   www.ryerson.ca/~dtudor/carcarr.htm
CorpTech   www.corptech.com
Countrywide   www.countrywide.com/chl_home/chlframe.html
CyBot   www.theartmachine.com/cybot.htm
Deadline Online   www.deadlineonline.com
DejaNews   www.dejanews.com
Department of Commerce   www.doc.gov
The *Deseret (Utah) News*   www.desnews.com
The Detroit Institute of the Arts www.dia.org
The *Detroit News*   http://detnews.com
DialogWeb   www.dialogweb.com
Digital City (America Online)   www.digitalcity.com
The Distance Learning Resource Network
                                   www.fwl.orgedtech/dlrn.html
The Document Center   http://henry.ugl.lib.umich.edu/libhome/
                                      Documents.center/psnews.html
Dogpile   www.dogpile.com
EDGAR (Securities and Exchange Commission)
                                   www.sec.gov/edgarhp.htm
EDGAR Online service (Cybernet Data Systems)
                                   www.edgar-online/
Editor and Publisher   *www.mediainfo.com/*
   Online List of Newspapers and Magazines
                                   http://mediainfo.elpress.com/ephome/npaper/
                                      nphtm/online.htm
Electronic Journalist FOI Resource Center
                                   http://spj.org/foia
Encyclopædia Britannica   www.eb.com
   Internet Directory   www.ebig.com
   Fee-Based Service   www.eb.com/search/
Excite   www.excite.com
   NewsTracker   http://nt.excite.com
Extempo   www.extempo.com
FACSNET   www.facsnet.org
FastFacts 1998   www.refdesk.com/fastfact.html
Fed Stats   www.fedstats.gov
Fed World Information Network   www.fedworld.gov.
Federal Reserve Board (in Washington) www.bog.frb.fed.us/
Fidelity   www.fid-inv.com
FindLaw   www.findlaw.com
The Fine Arts Museums of San Francisco
                                   www.famsf.org
Four11   www.four11.com
Fuld and Company   www.fuld.com
Georgia Tech Internet Surveys   www.gvu.gatech.edu/user_surveys/
The Guggenheim Museum   www.guggenheim.org/

The Hermitage	www.hermitage.org/
Home Path (Fannie Mae)	www.homepath.com/
Hoovers Online	www.hoovers.com
HotBot	www.hotbot.com
HotWired (*Wired*)	www.wired.com/newbot/
Hot News/Hot Research (Poynter Institute)	
	www.poynter.org/research/reshotres.htm
HuskySearch	http://huskysearch.cs.washington.edu/
IBM Patent Server	www.patents.ibm.com/
Inference Find	www.inference.com/ifind/
InfoGIST	www.infogist.com/
Infoseek	www.infoseek.com/
Inkspot	www.inkspot.com
Inland Mortgage	www.inlandmortgage.com/
Intelliseek	www.intelliseek.com/
International Council of Museums	www.icom.org/
Internet Lawyer	www.internetlawyer.com
The Internet Newsroom	http://www.editors-service.com/articles/ art98.html
Internet@ddress.Finder	www.iaf.net
The Investment Company Institute	www.ici.com
Jango	www.jango.com
Junglee	www.junglee.com
JustGo (Knight-Ridder)	www.justgo.com/
The *Kansas City Star*	www.kcstar.com
The Knight-Ridder (News Archives)	http://newslibrary.infi.Net
Las Vegas Sun	www.lasvegassun.com
Libraries (University)	
Bucknell Library	http://jade.bucknell.edu/
Case Western Library	www.cwru.edu/uclibraries.html
Dartmouth Library	www.dartmouth.edu/~library
Duke Library	www.lib.duke.edu/
Franklin and Marshall Library	www.library.fandm.edu
Gettysburg College Library	www.gettysburg.edu/library/
Harvard Library	www.harvard.edu/museums/
Iowa State University Library	www.lib.iastate.edu/
Marquette Library	www.marquette.edu/library
Ohio State Library	www.lib.ohio-state.edu/
Penn State Library	www.libraries.psu.edu/
Princeton University Library	http://infoshare1.princeton.edu/
Stanford University Library	www-sul.stanford.edu
UCLA Library	www.library.ucla.edu
University of Michigan Library	www.library.umich.edu
University of Wisconsin Library	www.library.wisc.edu/
Wellesley College Library	http://luna.wellesley.edu/
University of Waterloo's Electronic Library	
	www.lib.uwaterloo.ca/society/overview.html
Yale Library	www.library.yale.edu
Libraries (Law Schools)	
Cornell Law School Legal Information Institute	
	www.law.cornell.edu/
Brooklyn Law School	http://brkl.brooklaw.edu/

Chicago Kent–ITT School of Law   www.kentlaw.edu/
Columbia University Law Library   http://pegasus.law.columbia.edu/
Dickinson School of Law   http://206.102.94.190/
Fordham University Law Library   http://lawpac.fordham.edu
George Washington University Law Library
                                     http://128.164.161.3/
Georgetown University Law   http://141.161.38.45/
Howard University Law Library   http://library.law.howard.edu/
Indiana University School of Law   www.law.indiana.edu/law/lawindex.html
Loyola University Law School   http://157.242.152.7/
McGeorge Law School   http://138.9.150.10/
New York Law School   http://lawlib.nyls.edu
New York University Law School   http://julius.nyu.edu
Southern Illinois University School of Law
                                     http://131.230.102.1/
South Texas College of Law of Texas A&M University
                                     http://stexl.stcl.edu
University Law Center   http://stexl.stcl.edu/screens/opacmenu.html
University of California–Berkeley: Boalt Hall School of Law
                                     www.law.berkeley.edu/institutes/
University of Colorado Law Library   http://lawpac.colorado.edu/
University of Connecticut Law School
                                     http://137.99.202.99/
U.S. House of Representatives Internet Law Library
                                     http://law.house.gov/
Yale University Law School (Connecticut)
                                     http://130.132.84.29
Libraries (State)
Access Colorado Library and Information Network
                                     www.aclin.org
Alaska Division of Libraries   www.educ.state.ak.us/lam/
Arizona Department of Library (Archives and Public Records)
                                     www.dlapr.lib.az.us/
California State Library   www.library.ca.gov/
Connecticut State Library   www.ctstateu.edu/csl/csl_home.html
Delaware Division of Libraries   www.lib.de.us/
Georgia Public Library Services   www.gpls.public.lib.ga.us/
Idaho State Library   www.isu.edu/departments/library/helm.htm
Illinois State Library   www.sos.state.il.us/depts/library/isl_home.html
Indiana State Library   www.statelib.lib.in.us/
Kansas State Library   www.lib.ukans.edu
Kentucky Department for Libraries and Archives
                                     www.kdla.state.ky.us/
Library of Michigan   www.libofmich.lib.mi.us/
Library of Virginia   www.vsla.edu/
Maine State Library   www.state.me.us/msl/mslhome.htm
Massachusetts Library and Information Network
                                     www.mlin.lib.ma.us/
Maryland Public Libraries and Online Public Information Network
                                     http://sailor.lib.md.us
Mississippi Library Commission   www.mlc.lib.ms.us/
Missouri State Library   http://mosl.sos.state.mo.us/

Montana State Library	http://msl.mt.gov/
Nebraska Library Commission	www.nlc.state.ne.us/
Nevada State Library and Archives	www.clan.lib.nv.us/
New Hampshire State Library	www.state.nh.us/nhsl/nhsl.html
New Jersey State Library	www.state.nj.us/statelibrary/njlib.htm
New Mexico State Library	www.stlib.state.nm.us/
New York State Library	www.nypl.org/
North Dakota State Library	www.sendit.nodak.edu/ndsl/index.html
Oklahoma Department of Libraries	www.state.ok.us/~odl/
Rhode Island Office of Library and Information Services	
	www.dsls.state.ri.us/
South Carolina State Library	www.state.sc.us/scsl/
South Dakota State Library	www.state.sd.us/state/executive/deca/st_lib/
	st_lib.htm
State Library of Iowa	www.silo.lib.ia.us/
State Library of Louisiana	http://smt.state.lib.la.us/statelib.htm
State Library of North Carolina	http://dcr.state.nc.us/ncslhome.htm
State Library of Ohio	http://winslo.ohio.gov/
Tennessee State Library and Archive	
	www.state.tn.us/sos/statelib/tslahome.htm
Texas State Library and Archives Commission	
	www.tsl.state.tx.us/
Utah State Archives	www.archives.state.ut.us/
Utah State Library	www.state.lib.ut.us/
Vermont Department of Libraries	http://dol.state.vt.us/
Washington State Library	http://griffin.wsu.edu
West Virginia Library Commission	www.wvlc.wvnet.edu/
Wisconsin Division for Libraries and Community Learning	
	http://badger.state.wi.us/agencies/dpi/dlcl/
Wyoming State Library	www-wsl.state.wy.us/
The Library of Congress	www.loc.gov
The List	http://thelist.internet.com
The Los Angeles County Museum of Art	
	www.lacma.org/
The *Los Angeles Times*	http://latimes.com
The Louvre	http://mistral.culture.fr/louvre
Lycos	http://lycos.com
Personalization Services	http://personal.lycos.com
Martindale-Hubbell Lawyer Locator	www.martindale.com
MapBlast	www.mapblast.com/
MapQuest	www.mapquest.com
Maps On Us	www.mapsonus.com
MegaSources	www.megasources.com
Merrill Lynch	www.ml.com/
MetaCrawler	www.metacrawler.com
Microsoft's Internal Explorer (Personalization Services)	
	http://home.microsoft.com
Ministry of Culture and Communication (France)	
	http://www.culture.fr.culture
MLA-Style Citations of Electronic Sources	www.columbia.edu/cu/cup/cgos
MoneyCafe (National Financial Services Network)	
	www.moneycafe.com/moneycafe/stocfund.htm

Monster Board	www.monsterboard.com
Mortgage Bankers of America	www.mbaa.org/
Mortgage Market Information Services	www.interest.com/rates.html
Mr. William Shakespeare and the Internet	www.palomar.edu/Library/shake.htm
The Mutual Fund Café	www.mfcafe.com
Mutual Funds	www.mfmag.com
NASDAQ	www.nasdaq.com/

National Aeronautics and Space Administration (NASA)

	www.nasa.gov
Cassini mission	www.jpl.nasa.gov/cassini/
Europa mission	www.jpl.nasa.gov/ice_fire/europao.htm
Galileo mission	www.jpl.nasa.gov/galileo/
The International Space Station	http://station.nasa.gov/
Lunar exploration	http://nssdc.gsfc.nasa.gov/planetary/lunar/apollo_25th.html
The *Magellan* mission to Venus	www-b.jpl.nasa.gov/magellan/mgn.html
Mars exploration	http://mars.jpl.nasa.gov/
Mercury and Venus explorations	http://nssdc.gsfc.nasa.gov/planetary/planets/mercurypage.html
NASA's Jet Propulsion Lab	http://pds.jpl.nasa.gov/planets
NASA solar missions	http://umbra.nascom.nasa.gov/solar_missions.html
NEAR mission	http://near.jhuapl.edu
Pluto-Kuiper Express	www.jpl.nasa.gov/ice_fire/PFFinfo.html
Voyager mission	http://vraptor.jpl.nasa.gov

Wide-Field Planetary Camera 2 Science Team

http://wfpc2.jpl.nasa.gov/~idt/Favorite_images.html

National Center for State Courts	www.ncsc.dni.us
The National Gallery of Art	www.nga.gov/

The National Institute for Computer-Assisted Reporting (NICAR)

www.nicar.org

National Institutes of Health	gopher://gopher.nih.gov/
The National Library of Medicine	www.nlm.nih.gov
National Museum of Japanese History	www.rekihaku.ac.jp/
The National Press Club (NPC)	http://npc.press.org
National Writers Union	www.nwu.org/

The National Writing Centers Association Online Writing Lab (OWL)

www2.colgate.edu/diw/NWCAOWLS.html

Net Happenings Digest	http://scout.cs.wisc.edu/scout/net-hap/
NetSage	www.netsage.com/
Netscape	www.netscape.com/
My Netscape (Personalization Services)	http://my.netscape.com
Netsurfer Digest	www.netsurf.com/nsd

Networth Information Center (Quicken.com)

www.quicken.com

Neurostudio Inc.	http://isis.neurostudio.com/
New York Stock Exchange	www.nyse.com
The *New York Times*	www.nyt.com
NewsBot	www.wired.com/newsbot

NewsHound (The *San Jose Mercury News*)

www.newshound.com/main.htm

News Index	http://newsindex.com
NewsPage	www.newspage.com/

The 1997 Media in Cyberspace Study (Report)
http://mediasource.com

Northern Light — www.nlsearch.com *or* www.northernlight.com

National Space Science Data Center (NSSDC) Image Catalog
http://nssdc.gsfc.nasa.gov/imgcat/html/index/

The Official Internet World Guide to Electronic Styles: A Handbook to Citing Electronic Information — www.uvm.edu/~ncrane/estyles/

OneSeek — www.oneseek.com

The *Online Journalism Review* — www.onlinejournalism.org

The Online Press Club/Journalism Forum
www.jforum.org

Online Writing Labs (OWLs)
Bowling Green State University "Writime"
www.bdsu.edu/departments/writing-lab/
The Dakota State University — www.dsu.edu/departments/liberal/owl
Purdue University — http://owl.english.purdue.edu
Rensselaer — www.rpi.edu/web/writingcenter/
The University of Maine "Writing Center Online"
http://kramer.ume.maine.edu/~wcenter
The University of Michigan — www.las.umich.edu/ecb/OWL/owl.html
The University of Missouri's "Online Writery"
www.missouri.edu/~wleric/writery.html

The *Orange County Register* — www.ocregister.com
PCQuote — www.pcquote.com/
Phonebook Gateway — www.uiuc.edu/cgi-bin/ph
The Poynter Institute — www.poynter.org
The Practicing Attorney's Home Page — www.legalethics.com/pa/main.html
Planetary News — www.planetarynews.com/
PR Newswire — www.prnewswire.com
Media-Only — www.prnmedia.com
ProfNet — www.prnews.com
Public Agenda Online — www.publicagenda.org
Reporter's Desktop — www.seanet.com/~duff/
Reuters (and Other Wire Copy) — http://yahoo.com/headlines/
Rowe Price — http://troweprice.com
The *Sacramento Bee* — www.sacbee.com
The *San Francisco Chronicle* — www.sfgate.com
SavvySearch — http://savvysearch.com
The Scout Report — http://scout.cs.wisc.edu/scout
Securities and Exchange Commission (EDGAR)
www.sec.gov/edgarhp.htm
Shakespeare (James Matthew Farrow) — www.gh.cs.usyd.eduau/~matty/Shakespeare/
Shakespeare Oxford Society page — www.shakespeare-oxford.com/
Shakespeare Search Page (Massachusetts Institute of Technology)
http://www-tech.mit.edu/shakespeare/works
The Shakespeare Web Site — www.shakespeare.com
The Smithsonian Institution — www.si.edu/
Sidewalk — www.sidewalk.com/
Seattle Sidewalk — http://seattle.sidewalk.com
Washington Sidewalk — http://washington.sidewalk.com/

The Sistine Chapel (Michelangelo)   www.christusrex.org/www1/sistine/O-Ceiling.html
Smith Barney   www.smithbarney.com
Society of Competitive Intelligence Professionals
                                     www.scip.org
States.org   www.states.org
The *St. Louis Post-Dispatch*   www.stlnet.com
StockMaster   www.stockmaster.com
Supreme Court decisions syllabi (Cornell)
                                     www.law.cornell.edu/supct/
Switchboard   www.switchboard.com
Tate Gallery   www.tate.org.uk
THOMAS   http://thomas.loc.gov/
Travelocity   www.travelocity.com
University of Wisconsin—Extension (Distance Education)
                                     www.uwex.edu/disted/home.html
U.S. Court of Appeals, Federal Circuit www.law.emory.edu/fedcircuit
Virtual Reference Desk   www.refdesk.com/main.html
The *Wall Street Journal*   www.wsj.com
The *Washington Post*   www.washingtonpost.com
Web Bandit   www.jwsg.com/webbandit.htm
WebCrawler   www.Webcrawler.com/
West's Legal Directory   www.wld.com/
The White House   www.whitehouse.gov
WhoWhere (Lycos)   www.whowhere.com/
Writers on the Net   www.writers.com
World Wide Arts Resources Web Site   http://wwar.com
World Wide Web Virtual Library (Museum Section)
                                     www.comlab.ox.ac.uk/archive/other/
                                     museums.html
Yahoo   www.yahoo.com
    Yahoo Internet Directory (News) http://yahoo.com/headlines/
    Index of Internet Demographics URLs
                                     www.yahoo.com/Computers_and_Internet/
                                     Internet/Statistics_and_Demographics/
    Personalization Services   http://my.yahoo.com

Index

Page numbers for illustrations are in italics.

Books from Allworth Press

The Internet Publicity Guide: How to Maximize Your Marketing and Promotion in Cyberspace *by V. A. Shiva* (softcover, 6 × 9, 224 pages, $18.95)

The Writer's Internet Handbook *by Timothy K. Maloy*
(softcover, 6 × 9, 192 pages, $18.95)

The Photographer's Internet Handbook
by Joe Farace (softcover, 6 × 9, 224 pages, $18.95)

Arts and the Internet: A Guide to the Revolution
by V. A. Shiva (softcover, 6 × 9, 208 pages, $18.95)

Writing for Interactive Media: The Complete Guide
by Jon Samsel and Darryl Wimberley (hardcover, 6 × 9, 320 pages, $19.95)

The Interactive Music Handbook: The Definitive Guide to Internet Music Strategies, Enhanced CD Production, and Business Development *by Jodi Summers* (softcover, 6 × 9, 296 pages, $19.95)

The Business of Multimedia
by Nina Schulyer (softcover, 6 × 9, 240 pages, $19.95)

The Writer's and Photographer's Guide to Global Markets
by Michael Sedge (hardcover, 6 × 9, 288 pages, $19.95)

Your Living Trust and Estate Plan: How to Maximize Your Family's Assets and Protect Your Loved Ones, Second Edition
by Harvey J. Platt (softcover, 6 × 9, 292 pages, $14.95)

The Trademark Guide: A Friendly Guide for Protecting and Profiting from Trademarks *by Lee Wilson* (softcover, 6 × 9, 192 pages, $18.95)

The Patent Guide: A Friendly Guide to Protecting and Profiting from Patents *by Carl W. Battle* (softcover, 6 × 9, 224 pages, $18.95)

The Law (In Plain English®) for Small Businesses, Third Edition
by Leonard DuBoff (softcover, 6 × 9, 256 pages, $19.95)

The Retirement Handbook: How to Maximize Your Assets and Protect Your Quality of Life *by Carl W. Battle*
(softcover, 6 × 9, 256 pages, $18.95)

Please write to request our free catalog. To order by credit card, call 1-800-491-2808 or send a check or money order to Allworth Press, 10 East 23rd Street, Suite 210, New York, NY 10010. Include $5 for shipping and handling for the first book ordered and $1 for each additional book. Ten dollars plus $1 for each additional book if ordering from Canada. New York State residents must add sales tax.

To see our complete catalog on the World Wide Web, or to order online, you can find us at *www.allworth.com*.